1973

A Parents' Guide To

TELEVISION
MAKING THE MOST OF IT

A Parents' Guide To

TELEVISION
MAKING THE MOST OF IT

by Michael R. Kelley
George Mason University

A Volume in the
Wiley Parent Education Series
Mark Spikell, Editor

A WILEY PRESS BOOK
John Wiley & Sons, Inc.
New York • Chichester • Brisbane • Toronto • Singapore

Library of Congress Cataloging in Publication Data:
Kelley, Michael R., 1940—
   A parents' guide to television.

   (Parent education series)
   Bibliography: p.
   1. Television and children. I. Title. II. Series.
HQ784 . T4K44   1983   791.45'01'3   82-25620
ISBN: 0-471-87132-X

Printed in the United States of America

84 85 10 9 8 7 6 5 4 3 2 1

For Owen, again

CONTENTS

PREFACE

This is a book for parents, teachers, grandparents or anyone who worries about what nearly thirty hours of television viewing each week might be doing to children today. New research confirms a number of older studies linking violence on television with aggressive behavior in children and adolescents, and recent studies continue to question television's effects on children's IQ scores, their attention span and their socialization. Needless to say, much of this research is unsettling. Television is gaining a reputation as a powerful "drug" that keeps many of our children in a kind of mental stupor. Yet we all know that there's a positive side to television as well. It can be an exciting window on the universe, a means for children to explore the world and to learn about people whose lives are different from their own.

Like so many things in our world, television is best when we use it carefully and intelligently. It can be a powerful educational force in children's lives if we carefully select appropriate programs and make sure that children take the time and effort to reflect on what they watch. The purpose of this book is to analyze television's strengths and weaknesses as a medium that can both entertain and educate, and to suggest activities and topics for discussion that can make television viewing a positive learning experience for children. I also provide warnings about the kind of television viewing that can possibly cause real harm to children.

Although I keep up with the research on television and

have used it in preparing this book, I have purposely not written a scholarly book. Most of my suggestions depend on common sense, supported by my own experience as a radio and television producer, educator and parent. All that I or anyone else can do is make suggestions to help you understand a little more about the television medium itself. Ultimately, parents have to decide which programs and how many television viewing hours are best for their children.

I should note at the very beginning that I don't expect anyone who has full-time or temporary responsibility for a child to make the activities and topics for discussion that I suggest a constant accompaniment for each child's television viewing. No adult, regardless of good intentions, would have such patience, and no child, no matter how easy to get along with, would stand for it. My suggestions are guidelines and thought-provokers, to be used — like television itself — with care.

I want to thank my mother, Mary Kelley, who started my delightfully rewarding and long relationship with the magical technology of broadcasting by persuading me to sing on Washington, D.C. radio when I was four years old. And I want to acknowledge my immense and lasting debt to the late John Gardner, scholar, novelist, teacher and friend. John taught me how to write (though I still have so much to learn), and he persuaded me to write this book.

Michael R. Kelley, Ph. D.
Fairfax, Virginia, 1983

PART I: The World of TV

1

SOMETHING FOR EVERYONE

Today, a little over thirty years after television sets began flickering in living rooms across our country, more American homes have televisions than refrigerators or even indoor plumbing, and watching television has become the primary leisure-time activity for most of us. In three short decades, the television industry has reached its first age of full maturity. Now television is entering a new age of advanced technology. In the years just ahead, video cassette recorders, video disk players, cable television, direct satellite-to-home broadcasts, low-power television stations, home video games and household computers will make television even more prominent in our lives.

Television's great success has brought real worries for parents and teachers. According to the *Nielsen Television Index,* Americans between two and seventeen years old now watch television an average of twenty-seven to thirty-one hours each week, with children between two and five years old logging the most viewing hours each week. What does so much television viewing do to our children? Are children who grow accustomed to the fast pace of a program like "Sesame Street" bored by the slower pace of a classroom? And what about the content of the programs children watch? Is there too much violence or too much explicit sex? Are the values we want the next generation to learn presented in a positive way? Do our children realize the important difference between reality and the illusions of television?

We can take some comfort in knowing that philosophers and teachers as far back as Plato have also worried about the effects that the popular entertainment of their time would have on children. Although it has a "reality" of its own, fiction — whether in a song, poem, play, novel, movie or television comedy or drama — is after all only an imitation of reality. In every era thoughtful people have worried that a particular imitation does not accurately reflect the morals, ethics or religious beliefs they subscribe to, or that by altering reality, fiction distorts the values society esteems. Such concerns have caused societies in nearly every age to evaluate carefully the suitability of fiction and other imitational diversions, so that escape into a make-believe world might teach as well as delight, but above all, not do harm. Parents and teachers today have the same concerns as in former generations, but in addition to evaluating songs, books, plays, poetry, paintings and even movies, we now have to make decisions about the steady stream of television programs beamed into the home, often into the child's own room.

The worries are justified; the inherent dangers of television for children are real. But if we handle television with care, it can be an effective channel for learning in the home.

This book seeks to help parents and other adults understand how television affects children at different stages of their development, and to help you to use television at home for the good of you and your family.

Many of us have grown up with television, but few of us fully understand television's effects on us and our children. Certainly we know very little about what television has done to the American family structure, the American dream of success or to our own self-images. And sadly, we have made far too little effort to learn for ourselves or to teach our children how to view television with the same critical skills, evaluative habits and analytical questioning that we bring to newspapers, plays or movies. Yet most Americans spend more time watching television than doing all those other activities combined. The truth is, television has surprised us all, establishing its preeminence in our homes before most of us began to take it seriously.

EFFECTS OF TELEVISION VIEWING

In spring 1982 the National Institute of Mental Health published *Television and Behavior,* a ten-year update of the Surgeon General's report on television and violence. This report confirms much of what was in the 1972 report and underscores a number of points many parents, teachers and social workers already suspected. The report notes that nearly all of us watch television to some extent, but the amount of viewing time varies with our age, interests and educational level. Most children from age two to twelve are heavy viewers, watching television three or more hours every day. The number of viewing hours drops somewhat among teenagers. Young adults eighteen to twenty-five years old are fairly heavy viewers, with college students watching the most television. Then in the productive middle years, viewing falls markedly, only to be resumed in substantial amounts at retirement. Not surprisingly, most people who watch a lot of television aren't really busy; they use television as a time filler or as relief from boredom or loneliness, indiscriminately watching whatever comes on. College students are most likely to use the television set in a passive, mindless way to escape from the demands of coursework.

It's interesting that among adults some correlation exists between education levels and television viewing: Those with fewer years of formal schooling tend to watch more television than people with more education. Although the researchers don't suggest an explanation, the reason seems obvious. People with more years of formal education have learned to enjoy several forms of recreation and thus rely less on television. Among children, those with lower IQ scores watch more television than those with higher scores. Researchers aren't ready to speculate on why this is the case but no one is suggesting that watching television is the sole factor in lowering children's IQ scores.

Television and Behavior also summarizes the few research studies done on television's effects on the family, and calls for more studies on this important question. Although Americans watch some programs together as a family, television viewing is not a typical family group experience. There is little conversation or interaction, except for an occasional comment or two during the commercial breaks. Family members watching television together usually remain isolated from one another as they watch; they relate to the television set, not to other family members. In the 40 percent of American households with more than one television set, the isolation automatically increases. When family members do watch together, the grouping is most often that of a parent and a child, and in most cases the child decides what program to turn on, assuming the role of family arbiter. Finally, perhaps even more unfortunately, in the majority of families parents don't provide much guidance or control over television viewing. What guidance there is usually concerns the amount of time children can watch television, not what programs they can view.

With a far more frightening finding, the report confirms the worst suspicions of many parents and teachers: There is a direct correlation between violence on television and overly aggressive behavior in children and adults who watch that violence. Conversely, but not surprisingly, the report also cites research evidence that all of us can learn positive, friendly, altruistic behavior from watching programs that portray such behavior. Thus, ten years of social science research affirms what every parent knows instinctively and what Aristotle said in *The Poetics* 2,300 years ago: Imitation is a primary means by which all of us learn; from childhood through life, what we see, we tend to imitate. The implication for parents and teachers is obvious. Since children imitate the behavior and character traits they see on television, they should not be allowed to watch television indiscriminately and without close adult supervision. The risks are just too great.

In the face of these real dangers, some parents may be tempted to take the easy way out, going to the extreme of forbidding all television or limiting viewing to children's programs on public television. The problem with such an extreme solution is that it deprives a child of the exceptional learning experiences available from some of the very programs that children shouldn't watch alone. What we need is a middle ground, an approach to television viewing that is informed, cautious and moderate.

POTENTIALS OF TELEVISION

Before I suggest some of the ways in which you can turn your television set into a home tutor for your children, let's consider television in general, its strengths and weaknesses in particular, and why television has such potential for both benefit and harm. A glance at the TV program schedule in your local newspaper quickly confirms the immense variety of television programs. If you live in a community with cable television, the variety is even more staggering. If we look beyond the surface of the TV listings, however, we discover that there are really only two basic types of television programs if we define them by their primary purpose or intended effect: Those designed primarily to inform and those designed primarily to entertain. I should note here that few programs are either wholly informative or wholly entertaining simply because most entertainment is somewhat informative, and much information can be entertaining. I'm talking here about overall emphasis, not absolutes. Within those two broad categories we can classify programs by any number of schemes, depending on our needs. In each case, the classification for TV parallels the classification schemes we use for other media. We can classify television programs according to their intended audience (children, adults, women, men);

their content (tragedy, comedy, sports); their relationship to reality (news, documentary, fiction); their form (drama, quiz show, talk show); and so forth The point is, television programs in themselves are not mysteriously unique, different or particularly modern phenomena. Whatever classification scheme we use, television programs can fit alongside works of literature, history, art, music, drama and dance in the same categories that served in ancient times and continue to serve today.

What then is special about television? Why do television programs present potentially greater dangers to our children than works in print or on the stage? In one sense, the answer is nothing. Television is just a new way to deliver the same old things. Like the other communications media — recordings, radio, movies, telephone, newspapers and books — television repackages traditional forms of information and entertainment and delivers them in its own special way, subtlely altering the original forms by adapting them to the limitations of the television medium.

TV and Other Media

As a delivery system, however, television differs substantially from other media in two important ways. First of all, television is unique because it can bring words and pictures directly into our living rooms, bedrooms, kitchens, bathrooms and even our campers and boats for up to twenty-four hours every day. Think about that for a moment. In classical Greece, citizens would see plays and sporting events at special festivals held only a few times a year. Today, going to a play or a football game is still a special activity for the average American. It is a two-and-a-half-hour outing complete with excited anticipation before the event and the opportunity for critique and discussion after the event. Even going to a movie is a special activity, something to look forward to, plan and evaluate. But with TV, we can stay at home and still be bombarded with plays, movies and sporting events day in and day out. We take them all in by just sitting at home, passive, isolated and mostly mute.

When we experience the skills of artists or athletes, our minds should have time to reflect on what we've taken in and to digest and recombine our experience, insights and sense impressions. But television discourages this with its steady unyielding stream of programs. We sit in front of our sets watching one program after another without time to reflect, discuss or absorb. We are encouraged to "stay tuned" by the program promotions that accompany the commercial breaks. No other entertainment or information medium can do this to us quite the way television does. We generally use the other media selectively, pausing for extended periods to mull over what we've taken in. But television is a relentless, all-pervasive environment and a continuum of stimulation. In its presence, adults and children alike can become mesmerized; our mental circuits can become overloaded and overwhelmed. The only way to protect against such bad effects and use television sensibly is with moderation. Adults and children should watch television selectively and discriminately.

A warning to view television moderately seems too sensible to need stating, but sadly too many of us use television habitually and automatically without thinking. We use it to unwind, to put off dealing with family crises, to escape our troubles, to avoid feeling lonely or to brighten an otherwise humdrum day. In the process, we soak up more drama, sports, information, entertainment and creative talent in a year then people of past generations could get in a whole lifetime. What an opportunity gone to waste. By watching television in a self-induced mental stupor, habitually and without reflecting on what we view, we miss many opportunities to learn from this marvelous, magical medium.

Such passive, compulsive viewing may well be harmful for adults and children. We can be sure that youngsters who watch four or five hours of television each day without supervision, without asking questions and getting answers about the programs or thinking about one program before the next begins, are wasting valuable learning opportunities at a point in their lives when their minds are most open to learning. Every hour a child spends mindlessly in front of the television is an hour of educational opportunity wasted. Only when we interact with our children and their television viewing can television become a useful and positive learning tool for them.

Television's preeminence and its ability to bring all types of programs into our homes every hour of every day is clearly both its greatest strength and its worst weakness. On the one hand, television enriches us like no other medium, bringing the creative endeavors of some of the finest talents directly into our homes. On the other hand, because it is relentless, television can make even the most exciting event seem commonplace and ordinary. A glittering performance by Leonard Bernstein and the New York Philharmonic becomes just one moment in a steady stream of presentations. We know if we miss it today, there'll be another program like it in a few months.

The second major way that television (and radio) differ from the other media that deliver entertainment and information is in the use of commercials. Of the 1,079 television stations on the air in the fall of 1982, 802 were commercial stations, private businesses that earn their way by the sale of advertising time. It's impossible to underestimate the effects of commercial broadcasting on programming decisions. Broadcasting is the only medium in the world of art, entertainment and information in which the program products — the plays, the nightly news, the musical variety hours, the Christmas specials — exist primarily to be interrupted by advertising messages. This feature of commercial television has even spread to programs designed exclusively for cable television as well. Ted Turner's Cable News Network, Westinghouse–ABC's Satellite News Channel, The Weather Channel, The Health Channel and many more specialized cable television program channels expect to wholly support themselves by selling advertising time to sponsors. Because these channels get their revenues from commercials, cable television subscribers don't have to pay extra for them; the cable operators include these and many more special channels for no additional cost as part of the basic service.

COMMERCIAL TELEVISION

Since the average American family watches noncommercial public television only about 5 percent of the time, when most Americans think "television," they think about commercial television. So there's nothing more important for us to understand than how commercials affect television and its viewers. Because programs exist primarily to be interrupted by commercials, they absolutely must attract and hold large audiences to stay on the air. The larger the audience, the more people an advertiser can reach for less money. The "cost-per-thousand" of viewers directly controls the sale of network and local station commercial time. The station and the network that can deliver the most thousands of viewers for the least cost-per-thousand sells more commercials and sells those commercials for a higher price. Since it usually costs about the same to produce a program that attracts a large audience as one that attracts a small audience, the network or station with the lowest cost-per-thousand has the highest annual profit.

The need to attract a mass audience to television programs produces tremendous tensions inside the industry. More than the other traditional media, artistry and creativity in television must serve ends outside of themselves. Television seldom if ever presents art for art's sake; it presents entertainment and information for the sake of profit. Of course, book publishers, newspaper companies, magazine publishers and movie producers are also interested in profit and need to appeal to their respective audiences in order to be successful. But for the most part, each of these other media can profit well without attracting the mass audiences that television demands. A big city newspaper can be a financial success with a paid circulation of eight hundred thousand; a book is considered successful if it sells forty thousand copies; a movie is a smash hit if it sells eight or nine million tickets over the course of a six- or eight-week run. On the other hand, a network television program needs to attract more than twenty-five million viewers on a single night to be sure that it won't be cancelled. It's not surprising that the decisions needed to put together a television drama will be influenced by many more factors than the artistic demands of the story itself. This tension between the potentially competing demands of the program and the profit motive turns television production into a constant balancing act between often competing forces and interests.

To complicate things further, television's mass audience is not seen as a conglomeration of many different age groups and income levels. Each program seeks to appeal to the "right" age, income and education levels, to those people who make up the largest single segment of the population, have the most money to spend and tend to watch the most television. Many programs have been cancelled despite large audiences because those audiences weren't the ones that commercial advertisers wanted to reach.

Television and its critics have never satisfactorily defined the responsibility of programmers. Is it merely to identify and attract the mass audience they need for commercial success, or should television programmers also try to raise standards so that the audience will begin appreciating and demanding more sophisticated and intellectually stimulating fare? This, in turn, brings up the question of whether audiences really want intellectual stimulation from television. Much of what seems to be garbage remains on TV supposedly because the mass audience watches it.

In designing programs that will appeal to twenty-five or thirty million viewers, television producers try to include something for everyone in each program. As a result, there is often little of value for anyone. Producers want successful programs, regardless of whether the content of the programs is high in

quality. Thus, most programs appeal to the lowest common denominator. If a show is well-executed and the camera work,
acting, sets and sound and lights are highly professional — if the
show is a well-done version of what its producers intended to
produce and can get and keep the right mass audience, then it is
successful no matter how dumb or silly it might be.

In its quest for successful shows, television generally presents a bland, homogenized product; each network copies and
recopies the shows that work, and producers take few chances
with the new, the innovative or the experimental. Except for
occasional news specials or quasi-documentaries which overuse
shock value to attract audiences, programs are seldom shocking
because producers try not to offend any one segment of the
population or any special interest group.

But something is going wrong. The major networks are
spending over one hundred million dollars a year to develop
new programs, yet the few that get on the air each season are
attracting smaller audiences. Whether this is due to competition
from cable television, video games and computers, or simply
viewer boredom, the plain truth is that fewer of us are watching
network television now than in years past. The network executives know the audiences for each show are smaller, but so far
haven't been able to figure out why or what to do about it.

Federal Regulation of Television

Still another cause of continual tension within the TV industry
and between the industry and its public is the constant pressure
of the complex federal apparatus that oversees and regulates
television. Fearing that broadcasting, in its pursuit of profit, as
an unchecked monopoly might wholly ignore the public interest, Congress passed the Communications Act of 1934 which
established the Federal Communications Commission (FCC) as
the federal watchdog over radio, television and other monopoly
telecommunications industries.

Congress and the FCC require that broadcasters operate

their stations so that they demonstrably serve the public interest, convenience and necessity, and the FCC issues broadcast
licenses for a specific, renewable period of time. The Commission can revoke a station's license if the broadcaster has repeat-
edly failed to operate on the public airways in the public good.
Much of the news, documentary programming, religious programming and public service and public affairs programming
that we see on television is there because the FCC requires just
such a mix of program types to serve the public interest. Broadcasters must make equal time available to opposing points of
view when they editorialize or when they carry ads for politi-
cians seeking public office.

On the other side of this complex and sometimes grim
Consumer groups are cautiously watching to see what difference the recent deregulation of radio programming and the
new seven-year radio licenses will make to that medium's public
interest efforts. At the same time they are warning that television should not be similarly deregulated. The FCC now con-
tends that radio listeners will demand their share of public
service and special interest programming from the stations, and
those stations that don't provide what the public wants will lose
audiences, ratings and revenues. If this marketplace approach
works with radio, there's a good chance that Congress and the
FCC will try it with television, which still must walk a careful
line between commercial profit and the public good.

On the other side of this complex and sometimes grim
picture of the television business is television's overwhelming
commercial success. Programmers obviously must be doing
something right because millions of us continue to watch television. We may justifiably complain about inane comedies,
flaccid dramas, mindless game shows and sordid soap operas
(whose very name comes from their main commercial connec-
tion), but none of them would be on television if a lot of us
didn't tune in faithfully. Whatever their shortcomings, today's
television programs continue to deliver immense audiences.

To the great credit of many television producers, they have
successfully walked the fine line between art and advertising.

For every ten mediocre, forgettable programs each season, there have always been one or two remarkable delights. For every three spin-off copies, there is still the unique original. There is absolutely no reason why artistically excellent television programs can't be popular, or why something that is popular can't be an artistic success as well. In far too many cases, television programs have sacrificed art for popularity, but certainly not in every case. Television producers have done an especially good job in news and public affairs programs, for the most part successfully avoiding the temptation to let commercial considerations influence editorial judgments about program content. As a result, we trust television news and documentaries, giving them high marks for accuracy, fairness and lack of bias.

There are many ways to present programs on television. Public television often runs a four- or eight-week series, then follows it with another. Commercial stations have also experimented with the miniseries appearing either on several consecutive nights or once a week for several weeks. But experience has demonstrated that the best way to attract and hold large audiences is through a scheduling system that puts new episodes of the same show on the same night at the same time week after week. This is what built large audiences in commercial radio's time, and it continues to work well for television. But this weekly series format, relieved with repeats in late spring and throughout the summer, puts an enormous strain on the creative talent of writers, actors, designers, composers and directors. It's impressive enough to produce one half-hour episode of "M*A*S*H," but it's almost miraculous to produce over 275 half-hour episodes. We're impressed with an actor who appeared in ten or even twenty movies in a lifetime — for a total of forty-five or fifty hours on screen — but it's mind boggling to realize that Clint Eastwood appeared in over 192 hour-long episodes of "Rawhide" before he became a movie box-office hit. With this kind of demand on creative talent, it's little wonder that the quality of commercial television programs sometimes leaves much to be desired. Never before in the history of the world has any medium gobbled up talent and creativity the way television does.

But we should recognize that although the quality of program content is sometimes uneven, television consistently delivers us an immensely high level of professional talent. Actors, scene designers, graphic artists, camera people, reporters and sound and light crews — the whole technical and theatrical side of television — are almost always first-rate. Because over twenty-five million people may be watching a single program, there is a built-in demand for technical and artistic perfection. We have grown used to this technical excellence in our living rooms, and we come to expect the same level of excellence outside. Whether we realize it or not, television has made us a more demanding and critical audience. The bad effect of such constant technical excellence is that television has spoiled us for the community theatre, the college play or the local ballet. The good effect is that we can often spot an amateur on the stage and even a phony politician. Commercial television tends to make all of us sophisticated judges and critics.

EFFECTS OF COMMERCIALS

(Commercial television has affected us in still other ways as well.) For one thing we have developed internal clocks programmed for the interruptions of commercials. Our span of attention is now about eight minutes, and we've all learned how to maintain our interest across a two-minute commercial break.)Researchers need to collate the results of the many studies on the effects of TV commercials. When a child spends thirty-one hours a week paying attention to television programs that are interrupted every six to eight minutes for a two-minute break, does that child develop general habits of concentration that are also discontinuous? Will children come to expect built-in periods of interruption in all of their various tasks, from schoolwork to home chores? The answers we have now aren't absolute, but common sense, our own personal experience and the wealth of studies that we do have indicate that children who grow accustomed to the constant interruption of commercial television find it more difficult to concentrate for extended periods of time than those children who are not used to the discontinuity of television.

We all use the commercial interruptions to relieve the relentlessness of television viewing. When those of us with cable or subscription television watch uncut and uninterrupted movies, we miss the convenience of the commercial breaks and the chance to comment on the show, get a soft drink or make a quick phone call. Surveys of viewers constantly turn up the opinion that watching public television is "difficult." Of course, some of this difficulty, perceived or real, comes from the more serious subject matter of many public television programs, but I believe that a good part of that sense of difficulty arises because there are no commercial interruptions. When people watch noncommercial television, there are no rest breaks for the mind, no chances to get up and move around as there are when we watch commercial television. If all television were noncommercial, would we watch as much of it? Is the lack of commercials on public television one reason why Americans watch it only 5 percent of their viewing time?

The commercial breaks serve to jade us emotionally, however. Coming as they frequently do at the point in a story where emotional tensions are heightened, the two-minute interruption breaks into our feelings without giving us a chance to build to a natural and satisfactory relief. When a life-and-death rescue is interrupted by an inane skit in a supermarket designed to sell bathroom tissue, that rescue loses much of its emotional impact. When we return to the drama, our emotions are at a lower pitch than before and must be built up again. This emotional see-saw effect on our children through the critical years of personal and emotional development cauterizes them and makes them less sensitive to anything but the most hyped-up emotions. Subtle emotional highs and lows are likely to be harder to induce in many of those who have learned to take the commercial interruptions in stride.

Commercial television's need for mass appeal has also resulted in an emphasis on middle-class manners and values. Programs depict middle-class or even upper-middle-class families as the norm, and the rich and the poor as the exceptions, thus making the values in the middle seem more natural, more "American." Commercials particularly reinforce this view. People in commercials have attractive homes, good figures, exciting jobs and middle-class values. Welfare mothers don't endorse deodorants on TV; overweight women don't extol the benefits of headache medication; handicapped children don't fight cavities with fluoride. Commercials feature only the prettiest, cleanest, best dressed and healthiest among us. In the world of the television commercial, no one is an alcoholic or dying of cancer. Life's crises seldom go beyond heelmarks on a kitchen floor or a debate about which brand of facial tissue is softest. So it's not surprising that children who are heavy television watchers develop a skepticism about what they see on television. What we don't know for sure is just how far this skepticism carries over into a child's dealings with the real world, but we should be aware that it might.

PUBLIC TELEVISION

Up to now, I've been describing mainly the attributes of commercial television. Noncommercial, public television started nearly at the same time as commercial television in America with the idealistic goal of using this wonderful electronic medium to uplift and educate Americans wherever they live. With the passage of the Public Broadcasting Act of 1967, noncommercial television began its major growth to maturity, expanding its mission to include cultural, informational and entertainment programming in addition to educational and instructional programs.

Public, noncommercial stations get their revenues from viewers and from state, local or federal appropriations rather than from advertisers, and thus public television is largely free from the sponsor pressure felt by commercial television. Public television can provide a genuine alternative to commercial television, broadcasting innovative programs, taking a chance on creative talent, breaking new artistic ground and providing programs for large and small segments of the population without worrying about the ratings and the cost-per-thousand viewers. By and large the 277 public television stations have had some success at this. Public television has taken innovative programming risks with children's shows like "Sesame Street" and "The Electric Company," and succeeded admirably. Public television was the first to put tennis games on television and the success of that experiment made the commercial stations change their minds about the sport's drawing power. The public station, however, like its commercial counterpart, is still in the broadcasting business and needs to reach a large audience, particularly when it is seeking viewer contributions during pledge season. Many of public television's program directors select shows for their potential mass audience appeal, being careful to avoid offending, startling or angering the audience, just as commercial programmers do. As a result, public television gives us some alternatives, but also offers much the same kind of thing as commercial television does. The difference is often more a matter of degree than of kind.

CABLE TELEVISION

Today, with the growth of cable television, truly alternative programming has another chance to reach the audience. With thirty, fifty or over a hundred channels to fill, cable has the potential to offer something to suit the taste of various smaller groups rather than simply mass appeal programs. Yet, except for the Cable Satellite Public Affairs Network (C-SPAN), with its live coverage of Congress, and the children's channels, Nickelodeon and The Disney Channel, cable has so far given us a lot more of the same kinds of things we see on commercial or public television — movies, news, weather, sports. CBS Cable's Arts Channel, which provided fine arts programs similar to many on public television, folded after less than a year for lack of advertiser and viewer support. So far, the major difference between cable and over-the-air broadcasting is that cable gives us individual channels that offer one kind of program twenty-four hours a day, whereas over-the-air television puts a little of each kind of program on one channel throughout the day. Thus, cable has all-news channels, all-weather channels, health channels, all-sports channels and many all-movie channels. So far, cable's uniqueness is this ability to deliver your favorite type of program twenty-four hours a day.

2

THE GRAMMAR OF TELEVISION

Hard as it is to believe, an average American child by the age of twelve has watched over sixteen thousand hours of television. That means the average child has looked at television for nearly two out of those twelve years. In this same twelve-year period, the average child watches nearly a quarter million minutes of commercials. That's almost six months of commercials in the first twelve years of life. By the time this same average twelve-year-old graduates from high school, he or she will have watched another full year of television. That's one year of viewing for every six years of life — one sixth of an entire childhood spent silently, passively watching illusion and reality flicker across an electron tube. No wonder our children sometimes fail to understand fully the difference between real life and the illusions of television. And no wonder that some mentally disturbed children actually exchange the illusion for the reality or the reality for the illusion — shooting, stabbing or maiming parents or playmates in the mistaken belief that all would be well again after the station break, just as on television.

In the face of such statistics, there can be little doubt that we need to limit absolutely and firmly the number of hours our children watch television. As much as we all enjoy television's usefulness for babysitting, we can't afford to compromise on this. An hour or two a day is more than enough television viewing for preschoolers; no more than two hours a day is a fair but absolute limit for grade-schoolers and for teenagers. Some parents might bend a little for a special movie or sporting event, and maybe even not count the time spent viewing public television programs against the total. Whatever limits we set, we should make sure they are clear, consistent and enforceable.

Even when we limit its use, television remains a constant in our lives. That's why many researchers believe that all of us should become more knowledgeable about the television medium and more "literate" in its use. In order to control the television in our lives, we need to learn about television as an information medium and as an art form, and about its production techniques, program formats and ways of sending both visual and aural messages.

TELEVISION: THEN AND NOW

Those of us who have been around a while have had the chance to watch television grow up and become sophisticated. We know a lot more about it than our children, who today watch an entirely different kind of slick and technically flawless television. In television's early days, serious dramatic productions were performed live, and there was no way to edit out the goofs. In black and white and with inevitable snafus, early television had to struggle to create its illusions and often failed. I remember laughing at the absurd futuristic effects of "Captain Video" created from prespace-age cardboard, and I can remember sometimes being able to see the strings that made Howdy Doody dance. I can also recall live comedy shows where the pratfall didn't work and performers on stage laughed so hard that they couldn't go on with the show. And, of course, there were the many times when performers forgot their lines, bungled a cue or went through the wrong door on stage. I can also remember some of the terrible electronic glitches, when one of the big overhead lights would burn out and the stage would be plunged into shadow or when the microphone wasn't turned on and a singer stood in front of the camera, silently singing her heart out. We learned fast about reality and illusion in the early days of black-and-white television, and we need to teach those same lessons to our children today. They won't learn them automatically just by watching television, because today's pre-taped and edited programs are too technically perfect.

Today's child has no memory of life without television and no knowledge of any other similar medium that can help reveal how TV works. My generation had radio. I was ten when we got our first television set, a used seven-inch Hallicrafters with push buttons for each channel and a massive magnifying glass in front of the screen. In the early days radio competed with television, broadcasting comedy, drama and variety shows, so one could compare some of the same shows and stars on the two media. I can remember listening to variety programs with hosts such as Bing Crosby, Jack Benny and Red Skelton, and also watching them on television. Radio also had dramas like "Gunsmoke" and "The Lone Ranger," situation comedies like "Ozzie and Harriet" and even quiz shows like Groucho Marx in "You Bet Your Life" which all moved over to television.

But I was really disappointed when I first saw those radio programs on television. That little seven-inch, black-and-white screen ruined all my imagined pictures of what people and places looked like. Groucho was never quite as funny and out-rageous flickering at me from the Hallicrafters screen as he had been on our old Atwater Kent radio. Somehow he leered more on radio than he ever could in the movies or on television. Radio was always vivid and crisp and its pictures were for me clear and sharp. When I watched "The Lone Ranger" on televi-sion, Silver was not nearly as white and fast as he had been on radio. I also thought the television mask looked funny with its little eye holes. Of course I didn't realize then that by providing both words and pictures, television was reducing the demands on my imagination. Where radio and reading require all of us to aug-ment the words we hear or read with visual images of our own making, television cuts back on this imaginative activity, doing the job for us and, I believe, doing it less well.

But even that seven-inch Hallicrafters had a few things to interest a ten-year-old growing up in the 1950s. That small screen provided my first view of the United Nations General Assembly, and it let me see Senator Joe McCarthy play the role of congressional bully. And every single night for what seemed forever, I watched a six-inch-tall John Cameron Swazey report about the war in Korea and describe troop movements around Pork Chop Hill and the 38th parallel.

Those of us with whom television grew up were also absorbing its conventional ways of doing things. We learned to tell the difference between a live program and one that was on film or kinescope because the announcer told us what we were watching and we could see the difference in picture quality. We learned what a camera looked like because sometimes on a live program one camera would unintentionally show a picture of another. We also learned about two-, three- and even four-camera shows, and knew how to tell the difference. Because the boom microphone would get into the picture every once in a while, we also learned what it looked like. I used to imagine it moving around the stage over the performers like a little oval cloud. Every so often, we could see the studio lights when a camera angle got too wide or somebody repositioned a camera when it was still on the air.

TECHNIQUES OF TELEVISION

We also learned what can be called the grammar of television, the basic photographic and technical conventions and the rules for putting a program together. These are not something that everyone automatically understands. A television producer friend of mine made instructional programs for Vietnamese natives during the war. The Vietnamese would all gather around the one little village TV set and watch the programs, and once my friend was in a village when a program he had made was on the air. The show was about raising chickens; at one point the picture cut from a couple of chickens to a close-up of an egg.

Not familiar with the grammar of camera techniques, the Vietnamese thought they were seeing an immense egg the size of the whole television screen. My friend remade that part of the tape so that the camera started with a long shot of a farmer's hand holding an egg and then moved in close on the hand and the egg.

Many of us first learned this basic grammar from the movies, then simply added the techniques unique to television as we found out about them. But what we have come to know is mainly experiential. We've absorbed enough knowledge about technique to understand television, but we don't consciously know exactly what is going on in front or our eyes. How many of us realize, for example, that a primary difference in technique between movies and studio television is the number of cameras used to shoot the picture? Movie directors generally shoot discontinuously with one camera, then build a smooth, continuous flow of pictures by splicing or editing the various pieces of film together. On the other hand, television programs made in a studio and many produced "on location" use two, three or more cameras. The programs are taped as they happen, live and in real time, and the action is continuous from beginning to end. In situation comedies or variety shows taped before a live audience, there may be some pauses for costume or set changes and for special effects, but interview or talk shows generally run as close as possible to real time and news programs are done live.

Like film cameras, television cameras can zoom in from a distance to a close-up shot; they can be adjusted for wide-angle shots, telephoto shots and just about everything else in between. But television gets its dynamic movement range and picture variety by electronically switching from the viewpoint of one camera to that of another, not by cutting and assembling snippets of film shot by a single camera over the course of different days and at different locations, as in a movie.

This process of electronic switching provides the television director with the choice of several interesting effects. One picture can seemingly wipe another off the screen, gradually replacing it in front of the viewers' eyes. The picture from one camera can be inserted in the corner of the picture from another camera, and then expand out to fill the whole screen. By taking the electronic signals from the camera and putting them through a computer memory — changing them from an analogue to a digital electronic form — the pictures from the camera can be made to revolve, starting as a tiny dot and spinning out to fill the whole screen; parts of the picture can explode out from the center then recombine kaleidoscopically, finally coming to rest once again as the original picture. The special effects are limitless. Even the equipment manufacturers don't know all the possible combinations. The TV director also has slides, film or taped material that can become a program source and be electronically switched to replace the picture from one of the cameras or from the digital processing source.

Movie cameras can close the iris of the lens, shutting off the light and making the picture appear to fade. Television cameras do the same thing electronically with a slightly different effect. Simply by reducing the camera's video output from the switcher — much as you can reduce your turntable's volume through your stereo amplifier — the director can make the television picture fade to gray. With the addition of specialized electronics, the director can fade all the way to a solid black picture, then bring up another camera with another video image, seemingly out of that blackness.

These two completely different technologies impart distinctly separate visual qualities to movies and to television. We recognize the difference but don't always realize fully what causes it. The difference is further accentuated by the fact that live video and videotape both produce a less distinct picture than movie film, which has more visual information than can ever be contained on the TV's 525 horizontal lines. In video's favor, though, there are no smudges or link specks, no bubbles or dots left from the developing process. Perhaps the most obvious difference is that movies reach us through the reflection of a beam of light off a beaded glass screen, whereas television's images are the result of phosphorus glowing from the bombardment of an electron beam. Movies result from external light; television from internal light.

Despite these various differences, movies and television are similar enough that television has been able to borrow a great deal from movie techniques. Like the movies, television uses the fade out as a signal that a scene is over and the rippling image effect to introduce a flash-back scene. When one scene dissolves slowly into another we assume there is a shift in time or place. When the dissolve is "matched," dissolving from a picture of one object to a picture of a similar object — a mantle clock to a pocket watch — the picture itself acts as a way to bind the two adjacent scenes closely together in our minds.

Television has also developed a whole set of technical conventions of its own, many of them quick and cheap. Soap operas merely change the hue or color of a scene to indicate a flashback or a trip into some character's imagination or memory. Often soap opera directors add echo to the audio as a simple signal that the voice we're hearing can't be heard by other characters on the screen. News programs and even some dramatic productions use a split screen to provide a quick visual transition, eliminating the need for a verbal explanation or a transition scene. Sports programs provide instant replay as a matter of course, often with slow motion, and we accept the fact that the slow motion replay of the same scene will usually be from a camera angle different from the one we saw the first time.

We're now used to the wide-angle shot as a way of establishing physical relationships. Night after night, in news interviews and in live studio newscasts, we watch the camera start with a wide "two shot" — showing the news anchor and the weather announcer sitting next to one another at the table — then close in on one or another of these two people. We also see a lot of uses for the "chroma keyer" — the special electronic effect that can insert moving or still pictures over a specially colored backdrop on the set. Sometimes the picture fills what appears to be a large-frame screen behind the news anchor; other times you might see the weather reporter in a little box. After the anchor introduces the miniature person in the box, either the box appears to zoom out, or the camera seems to zoom in. In either case, the person in the box completely fills the screen and begins his or her report. With this chroma key box technique, even the television set can become a part of the TV production set. We frequently see hosts like David Hartman begin an interview with some far-off newsmaker by talking to that person's image on an apparently real television set. The technique has a reassuring effect, giving us at home the impression that we are watching television together with the show host.

Each of these techniques gives directors a chance to juxtapose images, allowing one picture to further define or comment on another. Thus television communicates on a subordinate, purely visual level. In a television drama, the director can reveal a character's personality by showing that character interacting with other characters, by having other characters describe the first character, by showing us the character performing certain revealing actions or by all the other usual primary means. But also, because it can juxtapose images, the electronic switcher allows the television director to reveal things about a character simply by cutting from one scene to another, thereby suggesting a visual parallel or contrast, a wordless pictorial statement that we often accept as even more objective than the verbal statements made on the primary level.

News and documentary directors use this technique all the time, and so do producers of commercials. With no more than a visual transition, a fade or a dissolve, someone suffering from backache at the beginning of a commercial can be shown playing tennis twenty seconds later with the implication — never stated directly — that the medication is wholly responsible. A political commercial may show the candidate in an open, trusting setting, holding a baby or shaking hands with workers at a factory gate, then switch to a shot of a smoke-filled room when the announcer talks about the opponent's views. Movie directors can also juxtapose images for similar effects, but because of its multiple cameras and its electronic switching effects, television does it much more easily, cheaply and often.

Effects of TV Techniques

We don't know what, if anything, these various camera and special effects techniques do to our youngsters' perceptions of reality. Most children unconsciously learn both the grammar of reality and the grammar of television in much the same way that they would learn two language grammars in a bilingual home. But just as some youngsters can experience speech problems, it's possible that some children may have trouble keeping TV-reality and at-home reality fully separated. Certainly we could minimize the chance for problems if we talked to our children about the techniques of television and how to analyze and recognize them.

In addition to what all of us have unconsciously learned about television's production techniques, we have also absorbed the whole panoply of programming conventions that television producers use in putting together various shows. Again, we are probably not consciously aware of how much we really know, because most of us don't think analytically or critically about television. We tend to accept blindly such incongruities as the audience applause when the star of a situation comedy first appears on the set. The applause shatters the world of illusion and jarringly reminds us that the program — which never shows that audience — was taped in front of a live audience. The laughter of that audience throughout the program is another situation comedy convention that we meekly accept. These shows also follow a conventional format. A set of stock characters reappear week after week. The individual characters don't really develop as the series progresses. Instead, each new program presents a new predicament or situation, and we watch familiar characters react somewhat predictably to those situations. Sometimes the situation or predicament is mildly funny in itself, sometimes it is potentially perilous. It doesn't really matter; the comedy derives from the characters' response to the situation.

Each kind of television show — serious dramatic series, news shows, quiz shows, talk shows, soap operas and action-adventure programs — has its own kind of formula approach, which we quickly learn and grow comfortable with. According to a 1982 CBS documentary, "Don't Touch That Dial," network producers have even developed specialized terms for many of these formula elements in television programs. Rather than caring especially about character development, plot, motivation or a theme's inner relationship to reality, network producers want to make sure that each dramatic scene has enough "top spin" — enough excitement in one scene to propel the audience into the next scene.

Producers also look for a "hook" at the beginning of a show, and at the opening of each segment after the commercial breaks. "Hooks" are situations or predictaments that will catch the audience and build enough instant interest to make the viewer want to stay with the show. When a program begins with an ambulance careening around a corner with its siren blaring, that's a good "hook."

Successful shows also have to display enough "heat." "Heat" is tension, argument or some other heightening of raw emotion that raises audience interest and (you guessed it) desire to stay with the show. When a new character appears, or when a show begins from scratch, writers are careful to see that they've put in enough "pipe" — the background history of each character leading up to the point where he or she enters the picture, or the background of the situation. In their first season, shows will often run through this background at the beginning of each program, usually during the opening credits. "Pipe" is laid down so it will be easy for you to grasp the story and the relationship of each character to the story.

In network comedies, characters always have to leave the scene with a joke. No one simply walks out of a scene. This exit joke is called a "blow" or a "button." So writers and producers carefully analyze the TV product to make sure that each scene in each show has enough "top spin," "heat," "pipe" and a few good "hooks," and that the comedy scenes end with a good "blow" or "button."

Formulas like this restrict and focus the range and direction of each kind of program, but they also help to create a sense of familiarity for us as viewers. Television programs have an inner predictability. We know when we tune in each week that we're not going to be surprised, challenged or made to work hard to be entertained. Television is an easy medium; we all know this intuitively, but we should learn to analyze the reasons behind that easiness and to understand why some programs are easier than others.

Television is now the primary source of entertainment and information in America. Teachers are right to want to expose children to other forms of entertainment and information — books, plays, movies — and it is understandable why they might not want to spend precious class time talking about television programs that students already spend far too much of their life watching. Yet the failure to deal with television in the classroom by teaching TV literacy leaves our youngsters unprepared to deal intelligently with one of the most pervasive forces in their lives.

Even before the inexpensive, half-inch video cassette recorders became available, schools could have included lesson units about television with study guides that students could use at home with their own television sets. The problem seems to be that for years the educators, like the rest of us, didn't take television seriously. Many of us still think of TV as popular art and consider its production techniques too contemporary or faddish for serious study. There have been exceptions, of course, including a program established by the Irvine, California school system. And we really can't blame the educators for the fact that there aren't more exceptions. For every new course of study that teachers add to the curriculum, they have to sacrifice some of the time used on other material that society and the school boards think essential. Either we prioritize continually, substituting one curricular element for another, or we must weave in new elements with the ones that have long been part of the school curriculum.

Television programs lend themselves to just this kind of interweaving. It remains absolutely essential to teach Shakespeare in our schools today, not only because of his inherent value but also because Shakespeare's plays can be a cultural and educational balance to the likes of "The Incredible Hulk." But we also need to recognize that children can learn a great deal about themselves, art and literature if they have to analyze "The Incredible Hulk." Why is it more like a cartoon than a serious drama? Why is it popular? Does it appeal to our natural tendency to root for the underdog, our collective frustrations with the hassels of life and our private fantasies that we can occasionally exert our own will on those around us?

TV's Stereotypes

Parents and teachers should encourage children to examine television's many stereotypes and conventional depictions of sexes, ages, races and various occupations. Although much research has been done to document the content of television's stereotypes, less effort has been spent on transferring the results of this research to classroom lessons that teach children to recognize the stereotypes and to understand them in a balanced and realistic manner.

As summarized in the National Institute of Mental Health's 1982 report, *Television and Behavior*, the research on television's content provides few surprises with regard to stereotypes.

to write

Television programs tend to depict male characters as strong, smart and ambitious, and women characters as sociable and warm, but often dependent on men. Overall, television presents more male than female characters, more youthful characters than senior citizens, more whites than blacks or Hispanics and more professionals and managers than blue-collar workers. Reflecting the American middle-class values, the world of television is populated by a majority of white males who are ambitiously pursuing interesting and exciting professions. White women, also in the majority on TV, are generally more concerned with home and family, though we are beginning to see more working women, some with interesting jobs. Still, more often than not, the television male gains financial security through work and the television female more often gains it through marriage or inheritance.

Television creates a convincing world for those who watch it constantly, but a world that is often menacing and frightening. Dean George Gerbner, of the Annenberg School of Communications, has made extended studies of the relationship of violence on television and viewer responses to it. He has found that because of the high level of violence and aggression on television, heavy TV viewers are less trustful and more suspicious of other people and believe — far more than light TV viewers — that the world is a violent place in which to live. Children who grow up in front of a television set, without parental guidance or comment to correct the oversimplifications or exaggerations that television depicts, surely have a distorted view of reality that is constantly reinforced by continued daily doses of television.

Because television is a mass medium and is geared to the common denominator of taste and education, television lags behind the cutting edge of social awareness and change, continuing to present stereotypical images that are stale and out of date. These include images of helpless, hapless young women, or crotchety, absent-minded old men. As a result, television operates largely as an inertial force against social enlightenment and change using a stream of images that reinforces the stereotypical *status quo.*

Until the schools make television literacy a regular part of the curriculum, you can help by questioning television's stereotypes and pointing out the technical tricks that make the television world seem more exciting, dynamic and slick than life at home or at school. Many of the activities I suggest in the following chapters can directly increase your youngster's awareness of television as an information and entertainment medium, develop analytical viewing skills and put television's "reality" into clearer perspective.

You can also help develop that perspective by arranging to take your youngster on a tour of your local television station and, if possible, getting tickets to the station's talk or audience participation programs. A ten- or twelve-year-old can learn a lot from looking behind the picture tube and unveiling television's world of illusion and fantasy. If you can manage it, take your child to a network taping in New York, Chicago or Los Angeles as part of a family vacation, and join the "live audience" that you hear laughing or applauding during your favorite situation comedy. If Phil Donahue comes to your area, get tickets for one of his shows. Wherever you go, make the visit most valuable by having your child pay special attention to the program you'll be visiting before you go to the station or the studio. Get your child to make a drawing of the show's set and write down his or her impressions of what that set might look like up close, what it's made of and so forth. Have your child take notes on the format of the show, special effects the program uses and on the performer or host so that he or she has a list of things to pay special attention to at the station. A visit like this is a tremendous learning experience for most children, helping them realize that television is simply one among many ways to bring people together and open avenues of communication.

Finally, with every single program your child watches you should make it a habit to ask why he or she is watching and what your youngster likes most about the show. These "why" and "what" questions make your child think about television as something more than just a natural, effortless, mindless time filler. Youngsters who have to tell why they are watching a program and what they like about it are going to develop a healthy, critical sense about what comes on television. They will eventually demand more from the programs or even move on to other forms of entertainment — especially if you listen to your youngster's answers and discuss those answers with your youngster. If you have more than one child, you'll also enjoy the different answers that each one gives, depending on their ages, interests and mental development. Also, children can learn from each other as they hear their siblings give different answers to the same questions and discuss the differences.

Asking "why" and "what" will also give you a chance to open lines of discussion with each child so, together, you can make better decisions about which programs are appropriate to watch in terms of each child's age, emotional maturity and ability to make independent evaluations. Because each child develops somewhat differently, we really can't apply any universal standard to all children of any particular age.

Parents who watch television with their children and talk about what they have watched can interest their children in seeing those programs from a new perspective, using selected entertainment, news, public affairs or dramatic programs and even the commercials to supplement and improve language skills, sharpen logical thinking skills, explore concepts in ethics and politics and augment civics, social studies, science and math lessons. Together, parents and children using television carefully can make it an invaluable tool for learning or as a private tutor in the home.

PART 2: Suggested Activities

INTRODUCTION

In this section, I suggest many activities and projects that use what we watch on television as the raw material to improve vital skills and abilities in three major areas: 1. communication; 2. creative imagination; and 3. critical and evaluative thinking. The purpose of these activities is to help children and even adults learn from their television viewing. Although I place each activity in each chapter under only one of these three general skills headings, a particular activity may well serve to develop more than a single skill or ability. For example, writing a jingle or song draws on communication as well as creative ability, but I group it with other creative activities simply because that seems to be the most logical place for it.

For the ease of parents and others who will be using these activities with children of various age levels and abilities, I've arranged the activities by age, with a chapter for children two to five years old, one for children six to eleven years of age, one for teenagers and even one for adults. In selecting the activities for each age group, I've been guided by the spiral approach to learning; activities in chapters for older children often build on and expand upon skills acquired from similar, but easier, versions of the same activities for younger children.

Within each chapter, I've arranged the various activities by categories of programs we see on television (including the ever-present commercials). In each chapter, I discuss and analyze these program types, noting things about them which children of that age are most likely to be interested in, and surveying the kinds of skills and abilities students at that particular age are likely to acquire from watching each type of program or commercial. Thus, as you read through the four chapters of this section, you'll find many of the same subjects discussed in progressively complex detail. I am, in short, following the spiral approach to learning with you, the reader, as well as in designing the exercises I recommend for your child.

I've tried to select activities within the major skills areas which roughly parallel the basic school curricular areas: art, music, language arts, science, mathematics and social studies. What I suggest can thus be useful at school as well as at home. Parents will find that many of the suggested topics for discussion can become topics for homework papers in one or another subject area, and teachers may want to assign some of these activities to their students as homework.

Finally, though many of the activities might seem to be geared to a standard two-parent family with one or two children, I've designed this book for a wider and more diverse audience. If you're a single parent, your child probably watches TV alone much of the time to avoid boredom until you get home from work. Though you won't have time every day to use these activities with your child, many of the suggestions I make can fill those special weekend hours you have with your child, giving him or her ideas to think about during the week. Knowing your child is thinking more critically about what is on TV will make you feel better about the fact that he or she watches more television than you think is healthful.

Grandparents, babysitters, child care workers and older brothers and sisters will all find that one or more of the activities in each chapter can keep a youngster happily occupied and learning important skills while watching television. Parents of handicapped children will also find these activities useful simply by readjusting the age level or altering one aspect of a particular activity.

One final word of caution seems in order. Remember that your children also need recreation, time for their minds to go into neutral, time to daydream and time simply to relax. Television can provide some of this kind of time; that is one of its major strengths as well as one of its major weaknesses. If you try to use every single television program your child watches as a jumping-off place for the quizzes, questions and activities I outline in the chapters of this section, you may find you have a justifiably angry child on your hands.

3

PRESCHOOLERS: THE DOING AGE

Children between two and five years old are a specific target audience for commercial, public and cable television programs such as regular weekday programs like "Mister Rogers' Neighborhood," "Sesame Street," "Romper Room" and "Captain Kangaroo," as well as programs produced by local stations. If you live in a cable community, you most likely also have the Nickelodeon channel, which shows children's programs all day, every day. Many of them — like "Pinwheel" — are specifically aimed at preschoolers. Television producers know the value of attracting these youngsters. When the viewing habit is established early, it's harder to break.

You might think that programs designed especially for preschoolers are safe for your child to watch, but unfortunately that's not completely true. Television programmers produce shows that attract the two to five-year-old, but are not necessarily good for the child. Television shows are a lot like candy or other treats. A little goes a long way and too much can make you sick. Remember too that each child develops differently, with unique emotional needs. There can be a world of difference between two five-year-olds. What one can handle in stride, another might find frightening or upsetting.

Think for a moment about those Saturday morning network cartoon shows and how some of them might affect a sensitive preschooler. Club-wielding cavemen stalk and are stalked by wild animals. Interplanetary visitors scheme to destroy two innocent young people. An evil coyote tries over and over to annihilate the hapless roadrunner, only to be squished, flattened, dynamited and nearly annihilated himself. This steady diet of fear and violence can scare the diapers off some sensitive little tykes.

Even a program like "Sesame Street" has come under fire from some researchers for its fast-paced cuts from one activity to another, its slick production and its high-intensity bombardment of the senses. According to critics, those techniques may make some children uncomfortable and may lead others unrealistically to expect that all learning will be similarly fast-paced and jazzy. Compared to "Sesame Street," a kindergarten class can seem pretty boring to some children, although for others it can be a peaceful relief.

Luckily, many two to five-year-olds don't understand a lot of what they see on television and may come away from the viewing experience less scathed. However, some images, characters or stories may strike a preschooler with great impact, remaining sharply etched in the memory unassimilated for days, weeks or even a lifetime. Some are a source of pleasure, but some are a source of fear and nightmares. To help guarantee good memories, you must control not only how much television you let your children watch, but also what programs you let them watch.

A preschool child should *never* be allowed to watch the following types of programs alone:

- Action-adventure cartoons with violence and aggressive behavior as standard fare
- Action-adventure dramas and movies with high levels of violence
- Medical documentaries or other science shows with detailed close-up photography
- Soap operas
- The evening news

It would be best if preschoolers didn't watch such programs at all, but we don't live in an ideal world. If your child is with you when you really want to watch one of these shows, you can minimize the potential for damage by commenting on the violent scenes. Put them into perspective, reminding your child that the program is only a story. When watching the news, try to put a frightening event into a more comforting, understandable context. If you know there are going to be vivid pictures of a plane crash or some other natural disaster, start some distracting game or conversation so your child won't see that scene at all. You must take control and exercise that control for your child's sake.

Even with wholesome children's shows, there can be no more valuable television viewing experience for your child than being able to sit beside you and watch as you point out amusing or scary things in the shows, answer your child's questions, comment on the action, ask your child what he or she likes about the program and fully share the viewing experience together. Television is a sophisticated, complex tool that can bring preschoolers more experiences with reality in four hours than their grandparents could have had in four days. That is both the danger and the delight of television and that is why you can't think of television as a pacifier, a babysitter or a time killer for your children.

Besides watching along with your child, you can suggest activities that will make the viewing experience more of a learning experience. Here are some of the things you can do with various types of programs, even commercials.

COMMERCIALS

Very young children naturally learn by repetition. Thus, since television repeats commercials over and over, preschool children respond strongly to them. Advertising jingles are often the first songs a child tries to sing, and product slogans may well be the first clever phrases a child repeats to show off a newly acquired facility with language. Children between two and five delight in playing word games. It's their way of exploring the limits of their emerging world, playing with the powers of language and testing out this newly discovered tool and its relationship to the reality around them.

Commercials on television often trivialize reality, reducing conversations between adults to apparently serious concerns about kitchen floors or deodorant soaps. Preschoolers love just this kind of silliness. I knew a three-year-old who would burst into giggles at the word "pantyhose," a word he had only heard on television. Another friend's four-year-old would sing commercial jingles unselfconsciously for her admiring parents, grandparents and the long-suffering friends of the family.

Like it or not, preschoolers are supersensitive to television's commercials. It would be nice if we could live in a simpler world where our children didn't display their talents at memorizing and vocalizing by repeating some silly slogans extolling breath mints or beer. But that's life in the television age. Luckily we can use our little ones' interest in commercials to some advantage by getting those little dramas to teach a variety of skills. All it takes is a little creativity and some time and attention on your part.

With preschoolers, the major objective is to get them to develop a healthy skepticism about what they see on television and to realize that commercials try to make us want things we didn't think we wanted. You can do this by explaining to them what is going on in commercials and having them participate in the same process through creative imitation and imaginative play. Commercials offer marvelous opportunities for learning, since children at this age are particularly attentive to the commercials' repetitions, their cleverness and combinations of words, pictures and songs.

Communication

- Ask your child to think up a slogan praising raisins or milk. Expect that your youngster will adapt a slogan already on television, but encourage him or her to come up with something new.

- Word play: Have your child tell you what words sound funny in a commercial and tell you why. Tell your child a word or two that you find funny as well and explain why.
- See if your child can pick out some words in a commercial that make the product appealing. What, if anything, do these words have in common?
- Discuss with your child the music used in various commercials. Do the songs make us happy or sad? Do the songs make us want to buy the product? Why? Does the rhyme make the words easier to remember?
- Invite your child to tell you what words he or she doesn't understand in commercials, then explain the meanings.
- Ask your child to take some of the words often heard in commercials and make up a commercial about a favorite toy.
- Play the part of an announcer in a "man in the street" commercial. Interview your child about why he or she likes peanut butter.
- Ask your child to name three things that are never advertised on television, then to name three things that are advertised.

Creative Imagination

- Ask your child to draw a picture of a favorite food.
- See if your child can name, then paint or crayon some colors that are in a commercial. Does any one color seem to dominate?
- Ask your child to sing the jingle from an often-heard commercial, substituting something that's free in place of the product name.
- Encourage your child to make up a song for apples, raisins or some other healthful treat.

- Have your child dance or clap time to the music in a commercial, then turn off the sound and keep the dancing or clapping going. Join in, with your own rhythm on a pot with a spoon. Create new tunes; repeat the rhythms.
- Ask your child to make up a commercial to persuade you to let him or her stay up a few minutes beyond bedtime. Reward your child if the "commercial" is persuasive.

Critical and Evaluative Thinking

- Explain to your child that commercials try to make things look better than they really are, then ask your child to compare a toy in a commercial with the same toy at home.
- Ask your child to watch a commercial carefully a couple of times and tell you some things the commercial does to make the product seem especially nice.
- Suggest that your child cut an ad out of a magazine for the same product or service advertised on television.
- Encourage your child to tell you why he or she doesn't like a particular commercial.
- Invite your child to watch a commercial for a toy he or she doesn't own and tell you the things that make the toy seem wonderful. Point out how many of your child's reasons come directly from the commercial, then explain that commercials are supposed to make us want something that we might not otherwise need or even want.
- See if your child can tell you why a particular commercial is successful. Together, list the ad's major characteristics.
- Point out that you can't always believe the nice man or lady in the commercials on television because these

people are simply acting a part in order to sell you a product.

STORIES OF ALL KINDS

"Tell me a story." These words have been spoken in thousands of different languages ever since little kinds first put a knee on this earth. Long before the inventions of writing, parents had passed the collective cultural torch to their children in stories told at bedtime, to soothe a bruised ego or elbow or to reassure a little one that mommy or daddy cares. Society communicates its values, hopes, fears, bugaboos, taboos, dreams and nightmares to its young in stories.

Until just fifty years ago, the storytelling was done face to face by parents, grandparents, teachers or siblings. Then radio assumed some of the responsibility for a couple of decades. Now television has taken over from radio as well as from parents, relatives and teachers. In the natural course of growing up, an American child today sees hundreds of thousands of little stories — commercial dramatizations, cartoons, episodes on children's shows, action–adventure shows and narratives. Television has become America's premier storyteller and is rapidly becoming the primary source of culturization of our children.

The stories our children see on television can affect them more than stories we tell them because the television stories have actors, pictures, music, scenery and dialogue. But television stories lack the personal touch, the opportunity for the storyteller to go back and explain or elaborate something a child questions or doesn't understand. So for younger children, the impact of television might be about the same as stories we tell them or even somewhat less. But whether you or the television are the more impressive and memorable storyteller, your television set clearly has a quantitative edge. You can never tell your child as many stories as he or she will see on television, and as a result most of your child's social and cultural formation will probably come from television.

Some of this knowledge comes from commercials and much from preschool programs like "Captain Kangaroo," "Mister Rogers' Neighborhood," "Pinwheel" or "Sesame Street." But some inevitably comes from the cartoons, situation comedies or action shows your child watches. The mind of a two- to five-year-old child is absolutely not equipped to fully handle most of what is on television. Yet amazingly, Nielsen's reports indicate that programs like "CHiPS," "The Dukes of Hazzard," "The Incredible Hulk" and "Roadrunner" are among preschoolers' favorites. But we all need time when our little ones are safely busy and out from under foot, and television provides a convenient, free babysitting service. Thus, a benevolent but wrathful green humanoid and a weird bird that lives through every sort of imaginable disaster, together with motorcycle cops and stereotypical rednecks, assume the task of passing the cultural torch to our children.

Preschoolers haven't learned how to distinguish between reality and illusion or to judge the propriety of various behaviors. At younger ages, children are indiscriminate imitators, and those who watch cartoons and action shows with violence tend to be, as you would expect, the most aggressive.

Whenever possible, you should carefully select which cartoons, comedies and action–adventure stories you let your children watch, remembering that preschool children aren't always sure about the difference between reality and story. Then you can turn those programs into positive learning experiences for a little one by building activities and questions around the programs.

These activities and questions can stimulate a child to think about what he or she is seeing on television and to be more than a passive recipient of visual and verbal stimuli. The child who interacts with stories on television is learning from them. Also, when you talk with a child about a program, you are likely to discover fears or concerns developed from watching a particular show. Try to vary questions and activities according to the particular program, always keeping aware of the child's developmental level.

Communication

- Invite your child to tell you a happy story. Write the story down and read it back to your youngster.
- Watch a program that features an actor or actress the same age as your child. Ask your child to tell you what it might be like to be in a television show.
- Watch a Dr. Seuss or "Peanuts" special with your child, then read from another Dr. Seuss book or from the "Peanuts" comic strip in the newspaper. Point out some of the differences between written stories and TV stories.
- When your child has finished watching a television story, ask him or her to tell you what it was about and why it was fun or not fun to watch.
- Ask your child to name things on television that aren't around the house — things like trains, horses or motorcycles. See if your child can find pictures of these in magazines or picture books.

Creative Imagination

- Encourage your child to draw favorite cartoon characters.
- Have your child draw landscapes showing the kind of terrain in which favorite cartoon characters might live; for example, the desert for Roadrunner or a tree for Woody Woodpecker.
- Invite your child to hum a familiar show's theme song to you, then vary the melody enough to make up a new song.

- Ask your child to draw or cut out of a magazine pictures of vehicles used in TV stories.
- Provide a photograph of a family member, preferably a relative who lives far away and ask your child to make up a story about that person.
- Clip some pictures of TV shows from ads in the newspaper's television section. Give these to your child and see if he or she can match them with the show on TV.

Critical and Evaluative Thinking

- Is the television program fictional or non-fictional? Explain to your child the difference between something that happens in real life and something that somebody makes up as a story.
- When a story is over on TV, ask your child how he or she might have preferred to see the story end. Is there another ending your child would prefer? Why?
- Ask your child what's funny in a comedy. What makes him or her laugh?
- Take some time to explain the difference between cartoon violence and real-life violence. The cartoon character aren't real, and what happens in the cartoon doesn't really hurt the characters because cartoon characters are just drawings. You can't hurt a drawing, but you can really hurt a friend or playmate.
- When your child expresses interest in an animal character featured in a cartoon or story, use this to introduce library books or picture books of real animals. Compare Mickey Mouse to a real mouse, Snoopy to a real dog, a cartoon bird to a real bird. Explain the animal's habits, care and feeding.
- If your child watches a show like "The Incredible Hulk," or some similar show which illustrates a person or a plant growing suddenly or changing radically,

discuss growth and change. Initiate a flower-growing or vegetable-growing project, starting with seeds that your child can plant, water and watch grow.

- See if your child can explain to you how the background music on a story show makes him or her feel. Does the music make the story more exciting and interesting? Why?
- Encourage your child to count the number of characters in a favorite story or cartoon series.
- Explain about child actors. Talk about acting, the process of learning what to say and imitating emotions (crying, acting scared, acting happy and so forth). To help your child understand the difference between real feelings and pretend feelings on television, have him or her act out a full range of feelings. Join in and make it a family project.

NEWS, PUBLIC AFFAIRS, WEATHER

News programs probably won't interest most two- to five-year-olds, and certainly no child that age should watch the news alone. Nevertheless you can use these programs to teach a preschooler several important skills that are particularly useful in first grade and beyond. Concentration, memory development, recognition of names, faces and places and some ideas about government and geography are just a few skills your child can learn from the news. You can help that learning by encouraging some activities and asking some questions. The variety is nearly limitless.

News, weather and public affairs programs in general are natural providers of information. Preschoolers won't understand much of this information, and it's just as well that they don't. Children at this age are in a "doing" stage, not a "thinking" one. Even so, some things will get through and make sense to them, and you can use those items to develop learning skills.

Just be sure to keep the learning process enjoyable for your child. Try to think of news games, word games or contests that challenge but are fun at the same time. Play along with your child and make the games a family endeavor. Here are some suggestions.

Communication

- Ask your child to listen to a news story carefully. When the story is over, see if your child can tell you what the story was about.
- Help your child to dictate a letter to the weatherman, describing what the weather is like that day at your house. Read the letter back to your child and see if he or she wants to make some changes.
- If you have cable television, watch C-SPAN with your child and see if he or she can recognize the congressmen's different accents. Help your child become familiar with accents different from those he or she hears at home or in your neighborhood. If you don't have cable TV, you can do this with regular news stories, particularly those that show foreign leaders speaking English with an accent.
- Make up a pronunciation game and see if your child can accurately pronounce some of the foreign names in the news. You could even have a contest with your child and some playmates the same age.
- Invite your child to pretend to be a news reporter and make up a news story about what a friend or playmate did today.

Creative Imagination

- Ask your child to name the colors of the news set and the colors worn by the news reporters.

- See if your child can draw a map of the United States something like the weather reporter uses.
- Point out buildings like the White House or the Capitol to your child when these appear in news stories. Then see if your child can find pictures of the same buildings in the newspaper or in news magazines, or even draw pictures of the buildings.
- Encourage your child to make up a weather report for a perfect day.
- Supervise your child as he or she cuts pictures of weather out or magazines — rainy day pictures, snow pictures and sunny pictures.

Critical and Evaluative Thinking

- After a news story on space exploration or space travel, see if your child has a toy that is somehow related to space exploration and travel, or can adapt a toy to make it seem related to space.
- In news stories from around the world, help your child to pick out plants in the picture that don't usually grow in your part of the country. See if you can help your child identify those plants.
- Ask your child to identify a familiar local potitician who regularly appears on the news.
- Ask your child to count how many different states are mentioned in a newscast.

SPORTS, QUIZ AND VARIETY SHOWS

Preschoolers may or may not be interested in talk, sports or quiz shows. Most will not be, since the natural interest at this age is in stories, word games, action and natural imitation. You may have a child who likes to watch play-by-play sports at this age or who enjoys the singers on talk and variety shows, but with the relatively short attention span typical of children two to five, the interest will probably not be intense. If your child shows some fascination for these kinds of programs, you can heighten the learning potential with a few well-placed questions and activities.

Communication

- Ask your child to name the various sports team colors.
- Have your child name various local teams and the sports they play.
- Pick out some game-related words that your child might not know — words like "huddle," "pass," "volley," "raquet," "dash" — and teach these words as your child is watching the things they represent on TV.

Creative Imagination

- Invite your child to color or draw a sports uniform used in various different sports — a basketball uniform, a football uniform and so forth.
- See if your child can draw a baseball diamond or basketball court. You might encourage him or her to draw a golf course, putting in lakes and sand traps on a rudimentary level.
- Play a simple version of one of the game shows with your child using ideas that your child would understand.
- Encourage your child to sing along with the singer on a variety show, or at least to clap time or keep time with a toy drum.

Critical and Evaluative Thinking

- Use a game show with contestants to explain the concept of winning a prize or succeeding in a contest.
- Explain the difference between winning a prize in a game show and winning and losing in a sporting event. One is an individual achievement; the other a team effort.
- Have your child cut out sports figures from the newspaper or magazine, and group the cut-outs by sport.
- See if your child can recognize various talk show hosts either by their pictures in the paper or TV magazine, or when they appear on television.

You should also encourage your child to watch a symphony concert or opera on public television. You can point out the conductor and even identify some of the various musical instruments. You can do this also with popular music performances in variety shows, pointing out the guitars, drums, horns and other instruments. If your child is watching a talk show with you, you might point out how adults let each other answer their questions without interrupting, and encourage your child to imitate that polite practice.

Learning takes place whenever you encourage your children to interact with what they watch on television rather than to absorb visual and sound images passively. For preschoolers, such passive absorption is particularly dangerous, because their minds are already poised to learn about the world around them by taking in everything and absorbing whatever they experience. Television bombards these sensitive, unformed minds and overloads the circuits. Preschoolers can't process the information quickly or precisely enough to make sense of it all. By limiting viewing hours and carefully monitoring the programs your child views during those limited hours, and — most importantly — by taking the time to help your child interact with the programs he or she views, you can control the levels of stimulation. You can help your child learn to deal with the material coming in to his or her brain.

Television can bring a wealth of exciting ideas, images and stimulations to a preschooler's mind. You have to regulate the flow and content so that it matches your child's ability to get the most out of these exciting opportunities.

4

THE GRADE SCHOOL YEARS

Six- to eleven-year-olds are at an exciting learning stage. They're particularly ripe for the kind of broadening experiences that television's pictures and sounds can provide. The reverse side of this, of course, is that there's a great temptation for children at this age to make television viewing a full-time habit. Unlike the younger child whose concentration span is shorter, the six- to eleven-year-old mind is maturing by increasing its powers of concentration and reasoning. As a young mind improves its ability to stick with a task to completion, television can make an insidious appeal, holding the grade schooler like glue. Habits formed at this age are hard to break. Bad television viewing habits are even more devastating in high school, where youngsters need time for homework and other leisure-time activities. Habitual television viewers can miss out on socialization opportunities; although they get certain kinds of mental stimulation from television, the overall effect of constant, habitual television viewing is negative.

Controlled, careful use of television by children at this age can give them enormous benefits, which can be increased if parents encourage their children to think about the programs rather than just vegetating in front of the set. Let's look at some activities that can raise your child's media literacy level and make television work as a teacher.

COMMERCIALS

Because television has so many commercials and repeats them so often, and because children are better at remembering individual scenes or events than the links between scenes, commercials (which are nothing more than separate little scenes) can impress and affect a gradeschooler more than anything else on television. Your child has also probably become pretty savvy about commercials, recognizing that products often don't live up to advertising claims and that commercials use all kinds of verbal and visual tricks to make their products look better than they really are. By the time children get to grade school, they have become fairly sophisticated critics of commercials. At age six or seven, your child might not yet be ready for all of the kinds of analysis I suggest in the following activities, but by age eight or nine, most children are ready to look behind the commercials to see how they work.

You can help your child to understand the power of commercials by questioning each of the commercial's claims, by reminding your child how different a televised toy looks in real life and by pointing out some of the basic tricks that commercials use to persuade us to buy a particular product or service. Point out, for example, that some commercials try to associate their products with attractive people, places or activities. Other commercials persuade by encouraging the viewer to join the crowd that's switching to the particular product. Some use famous people to endorse the product; other commercials do just the opposite, showing what appear to be just ordinary folks using the product and praising its value. Point out, as well, that almost all commercials use certain words that allow the commercial to praise a product without going out on a limb — words that appear to make positive claims for a product, but which really don't say that much at all. Commercials frequently contain words like: "virtually," "usually," "most," "nearly everyone," "chances are," "might" and "often." These words sound like they are positive and forceful, but they really don't say that much for the product.

You might also want to point out that commercials make an art of using fancy settings, sincere, attractive people, supposed experts in a field, and catchy jingles and slogans. Whatever you can do to get your child to look beyond the surface of the commercials, to find out how they work and why they seem so convincing, helps develop critical viewing skills that your child can use with other programs, as well as in other endeavors.

Communication

- Ask your child to list three commercials that use the words "science" and/or "scientist" to help sell a product. Is this true science or simply one kind of hype?
- Have your child make a list of major advantages that a commercial claims for its product. Do this with a number of commercials and notice how often the same benefits or advantages are claimed about competing products.
- Ask your child to keep a log of how many times certain words are spoken in each commercial — words like "new," "improved," "better" or "bigger." What makes these words useful in commercials?
- Now ask your child to log words that commercials use to hedge their claims — words like "most," "may," "usually," "nearly everyone" and "often." See if your child can discover other words like these in commercials.
- Encourage your child to use some of the words often found in commercials to make up a public service announcement persuading people not to litter the parks. Explain in the process that public service announcements are messages of benefit to the community

which broadcasters provide free of charge in the public interest.

- We live in a new, high-technology age. Though many people are not sure exactly what the words mean, commercials often claim that their products are better because of "new technological breakthroughs." Ask your child to find commercials that use words like "technology," "electronics" and "computers" to make special claims for their products. See if your child can tell you why commercials use these kinds of words when many people watching the commercials don't know exactly what the words mean.

Creative Imagination

- Have your child draw four or five boxes, and inside each box set out the basic scene of a commercial for apple sauce or a similar natural food treat. Write under each box a short description of what will go on in the scene and what the characters will say.
- Encourage your child to draw a picture of a favorite food or toy and make it look especially attractive just as commercials do.
- Invite your child to make up a commercial to get you to do something like raise his or her allowance or go out to the movies as a family.
- Challenge your child to choose something totally useless, like a rock, a broken toy or a dead twig, and using all the tricks of television commercials, make up a commercial that will convince you that you must have that useless item.
- Ask your child to make up a rhyming song about milk, eggs or some other staple.
- Have your child draw a picture of a vegetable in its natural state and the same vegetable as it might be presented on the table in a commercial. A variation

on this is to have your child find pictures in a magazine of a vegetable on the farm and the same vegetable in a frozen food ad. Why does the commercial change the way things look?

- See if your child can explain how various colors are used to make a product attractive or to create a certain mood in the commercial.

Critical and Evaluative Thinking

- Invite your child to watch a commercial carefully, then point out some of the visual techniques — camera shots, graphics, colors — that the commercial uses to make its product attractive and appealing.
- Help your child to keep a log of the types of products advertised on TV such as household products, toys, things to eat, things to drink and medicines. Make a bar graph to illustrate which category of products has the most commercials.
- Ask your child to identify three "ethnic" foods advertised on television.
- See if your child can find three commercials on TV which use a foreign country as the setting to sell a product or service.
- Have your youngster count up the number of commercial minutes in an hour show. Figuring that there are three hours of prime time each night, ask your child to estimate how many one-minute commercials will be on prime time television in a week.
- Help your child to reduce the major argument of a commercial to its basic major points. For example, "You should buy this car because it is . . . ."
- The next time your child asks you to buy something seen advertised on television, ask why you should buy the item. Then look at the commercial for that item together and see how many of your child's reasons

are the same as those used in the commercial. Point out how commercials plant ideas in our heads in order to persuade us to want things or do things. After explaining all this, ask your child if he or she still really wants you to buy the item.

- Select three commercials that use well-known stars to sell a product and ask your child if there is any link between the star and the product. If you can't find an obvious link, see if your child can tell you why the commercial uses the star to endorse the product.

- You can use various commercials to encourage your child to think about the persuasive process more analytically, if you ask:

    1. Who is the main speaker/persuader in the commercial?
    2. What product is being sold?
    3. Why are we supposed to want the product?
    4. How does the commercial make us feel about the product?

    Don't expect answers to each question for every commercial.

- Ask your child to give you one or two reasons why music is used in various commercials.

STORIES OF ALL KINDS

Like their younger brothers and sisters, children in grade school enjoy hearing and seeing stories that are either funny or that feature action and adventure. First-, second- and third-graders don't remember the details of stories as well as older children, but both younger and older children understand and remember more of what they see when you provide some explanation and analysis to help them tie together the separate parts of a story. Much of what children watch on television is high in action but light in motivation or character development. Characters are often one-dimensional, being either total villians or complete heroes. The emphasis is on the action, and the reasons why people in the stories do what they do may never come across. Again, you can help your child improve his or her understanding by commenting on the characters and suggesting why a character might have acted in a certain way.

Even in television programs that don't have much action, many characters are narrowly and flatly drawn. In situation comedies, for example, our pleasure comes in part from watching a well-known type of character in a variety of comic or absurd situations. If both the character and the situation kept changing from program to program, the comedy would be less effective. In cartoons, the characters' personalities are nearly as flat as the drawing surface itself. Why, for example, does the coyote want to destroy the roadrunner? Why, in the face of such apparently unjustified animosity, isn't the roadrunner emotionally drained and depressed? Questions like these are absurd when we ask them about a cartoon character, but they're nearly as absurd when we ask them about characters in many situation comedies as well. Often the only answer to a character's motivation is simply, "That's the way it is." It's important for your child to understand and realize that in many television programs there's little logic behind what the characters do and say.

It's especially valuable to make clear to children in grade school which stories are "real" and which are make-believe. This distinction is clearer with cartoon stories, but even there it's best to remind younger children that they're watching only a story. Remember too that although children learn important things from stories, watching stories every day for hours at a time severely limits a child's ability to learn other useful things. Children need a lot more than stories to help them grow. By encouraging your child to interact with the programs on various levels, you can make those comedy and adventure programs that your child does watch a little more than simple time fillers.

Many of the features in television situation comedies and action dramas are the same as in novels and plays. A child who can distinguish the elements of story (characters, dialogue, setting, scenery and costumes) and can make judgments about why he or she likes or dislikes a particular program is practicing some of the same critical skills teachers want children to learn in English classes. Older children can even deal with questions of character motivation and realism in these programs, as well as discuss the difference between programs that simply entertain and programs that interrupt the entertainment to teach some social or moral lesson.

Although I've said it more than once already, let me say it again: Comedies and action dramas with high levels of violence and aggression directly affect your child's level of personal aggression and sense of well-being. Children who consistently watch violence-ridden television programs naturally tend to imitate what they see, and understandably perceive the world as a more violent and aggressive place in which to live than children who see little violence on television. Monitor what your child watches on television; be firm in sticking to decisions you make about what programs your children can and cannot watch. It is far easier to head off the possibility of damage before it happens than to try to repair it after it has happened.

Communication

- Encourage your child to write or tell you a story about a favorite television character. Ask what happens first, then what happens next.
- Ask your child to tell you why he or she liked a particular story on TV, then write a letter about the show to the network or local station programming department (network addresses are in the appendix to this book).
- Now ask your child to tell you why he or she didn't like a particular show on TV, and write a letter about

that to the network or local station programming department.

- Select a television show based on a short story or novel (often this information will be in the newspaper's television selection preview of the show). Have your child watch the show, then read the book and tell you some of the differences. Explain a little about the differences and that television often compresses the story, focusing on actions rather than dealing in a more leisurely way with background details. Point out that in TV there is no narrator; characters speak directly to one another, and we can watch what they do.

- Teach your youngster the habit of writing down words he or she doesn't understand while watching television. Help your child to look those words up in the dictionary.

- As you and your child watch a TV drama or comedy show, ask your child to pick out points in the story where what one of the characters does seems "out of character" or illogical within the framework of the story itself.

- Encourage your youngster to make up the ending to a story about a scientist who after twenty years of research and much failure finally finds a cure for some dread disease.

- Explain to your youngster that a plot is simply a sequence of events or actions that together make up a story. Then encourage him or her to pick out the major events in a TV drama and summarize the plot.

Creative Imagination

- Have your child keep track of what stays the same from week to week in a favorite situation comedy or action story. Keep a list of those things — the characters, the set or locale and the basic kind of story line. Then invite your youngster to write or dictate to you an outline for an episode of the show, making sure to include those things that are the same in the show each week.

- Ask your youngster to pretend that a favorite character from one TV series is making a guest appearance on another and to write a scenario of what would happen. What if Hawkeye made a guest appearance on "Diff'rent Strokes" or Alice showed up on "One Day at a Time?"

- See if your child can tell you how a favorite show might change if it had a different racial or sexual focus. What would have to change if "The Jeffersons" were a Puerto Rican family or if "One Day at a Time" involved a divorced father with two teen-age sons?

- Have your child pretend to be a character in a favorite comedy show. Ask him or her to identify and mimic that character's major traits.

- Invite your child to draw a favorite cartoon or dramatic character. Make up a different wardrobe for the character to fit different weather conditions, different activities and different situations. Encourage your child to draw himself or herself into the new situations as well.

- With books from the library, let your child find pictures of various kinds of housing — prairie housing, mountain housing, city housing and so forth. Compare these to the houses shown in "Little House on the Prairie," "The Waltons" and "Archie Bunker's Place." Encourage your child to design other houses for these shows.

- Explain to your child that every movement for every cartoon character is made up of a sequence of drawings. Get a pad of paper and have your child draw figures on each page, then flip through the pad to see the movement effect. With a little practice and a lot of pads your child can do some pretty impressive things with this.

- Have your child think up some funny situation or exciting adventure that could be the center piece for an episode on a favorite program. Then have your child write it up and send it to the program's executive producer, in care of the Network's address that you'll find in the appendix of this book.
- Select a TV situation comedy. Have your child imagine what various members of your family would do in that situation.
- Ask your child to make up a science fiction episode featuring a woman scientist as the main character.

Critical and Evaluative Thinking

- Point out to your child how some situation comedies teach lessons through their humor, then ask when a show is teaching and when it is entertaining.
- Help to get your child to think about stereotyped characters. Ask if he or she thinks all Southerners are like the characters in the "Dukes of Hazzard" or if all divorced mothers are like Ann Romano in "One Day at a Time." Are all gradeschoolers smart and scheming like Gary Coleman in "Diff'rent Strokes?"
- Explain to your child why catastrophes in cartoons and some situation comedies seem funny when they wouldn't seem funny at all if they happened to people in real life.
- Suggest that your child take a poll among friends or the whole class at school. Find out each one's three favorite shows. Transfer the information to a bar graph to show the most popular shows. Then ask

your child to explain why his or her friends and class-mates like a particular show best.

- Ask your child to select a favorite TV character in a series. Then, each week make a list that includes things the character often wears, things the character frequently says, things the character often does and a place where the character is often found.
- Have your youngster keep a list of the various ani-mals, insects and plants he or she sees on television in one full week of viewing. Include cartoon and puppet animals as well. Are there certain animals, plants and insects featured most often? Is there any apparent reason for that?
- Ask your child to keep a log of how many hours each day he or she watches television, noting what kinds of programs are watched the most. Count situation com-edies, action adventure stories and dramas as one kind and group them as "stories." Are stories the most popular kind of program?
- See if your child can tell you the underlying message or theme of a particular episode of a dramatic or comedy series.

NEWS, PUBLIC AFFAIRS, WEATHER

As your children grow older, they become more interested in what schools call current events. News, public affairs and weath-er programs convey a range of information that children will have to analyze and learn to understand as they grow toward adulthood. You can focus the natural learning process so that it is more efficient, helping children to organize some of the wealth of information by your questions and the activities you suggest. Watching the news with your child also allows you to answer questions and calm fears that your child might develop in response to particularly horrible stories. Children between six and eleven are still too young and impressionable to watch the news alone without an adult nearby.

Most television stations and all the networks will usually warn you before they broadcast something particularly gruesome, so that you can prevent your children from watching. Aside from rare scenes that may upset viewers, most television news and information programs can be sources of valuable learning experience for youngsters in grade school. They can provide lessons in history, civics, social studies and geography and parents can give these even more meaning by providing background explanations, answering questions and suggesting further source materials and related activities.

Communication

- Ask your child to write or dictate a news story about something that happened at school. Include "made-up" quotes from those involved in the event at school.
- Suggest that your youngster keep a count of the local news stories on your local station or the national news stories on one of the network's nightly half-hours. How many stories are about events and how many simply report on statements by local or national government spokesmen?
- Working with the local weather forecasts on the television and with a good dictionary, help your child to understand the basic weather terms: cold front, high-pressure area, low-pressure area, barometer, humidity, tornado and hurricane.
- If you have cable television, your children can play C—SPAN. With a friend or another family member, children can stage mock debates like they see in Congress. Have the children choose up sides and let the best argument win.

- See how many local, state and national officials your child can name: Mayors, Governors, Representatives and Senators.
- Remember that TV brings news about science, space exploration and everything that is new and fast-breaking in the scientific field much more rapidly than school texts, which lag at least a year or so behind. Encourage your youngster to watch news coverage of space take-offs, landings and other scientific breakthroughs. Encourage your child to look up new and unfamiliar terms either in the dictionary or in an encyclopedia at the library or at school.
- Encourage your child to practice pronouncing foreign place names and names of people in the news.
- If you have a recorded weather forecast on the phone in your community, have your child dial the weather and copy down the forecast. With this information, suggest that your child work up a weather forecast like the one on TV, adding some extra facts and even making up some background information to augment the forecast provided over the phone.
- Point out to your child the way the news announcers pronounce everything carefully and clearly. Help your youngster to become aware of this kind of precise pronunciation and to use it as a model for his or her pronunciation.
- Play capitals: Name American states or foreign countries and see how many capital cities your child knows.
- Play national leaders: Name foreign countries and see how many national leaders your child can name.

Creative Imagination

- Watch the news with your child and help him or her to tell you each time there's a switch from one camera to another in the studio, and when a camera "on the scene" outside the studio is taking its picture from a new angle or point of view.

- Play pretend. Suggest that your child join some friends and put on a mock news program. Have someone do the news, someone else do the weather and someone else do the sports. If there are enough children, there can be on-the-scene reporters as well. Get the children to make up the stories. If you have audio or video cassette recorders, you could tape the news so the children can critique their work.

- Ask your child to tell you what he or she would like to be — some ruler or other newsmaker. As that person, what would your child do to make news?

- Suggest that your child draw an outline map of the United States and put your hometown on the map. Ask him or her to draw in rain, clouds and snow, using the kind of weather each area might be having that day.

- Ask your child to make up several "good news" stories about special events in school, community or home; then ask him or her to explain why these kinds of stories should be on the television news more often.

- Do your local stations have theme music for their newscasts? Have your child compare a program with music and one without music. What does music add? Is it effective?

Critical and Evaluative Thinking

- Introduce the following questions: What is the possible intent of the news director in choosing a particular news item? What is the possible effect of that news item? What techniques are employed in presenting the story. It's especially instructive to realize that different news organizations handle the same day's news differently.

- If you have cable television, you can have your child watch a news sequence on Cable News Network and on the Westinghouse Satellite News Channel, then compare the handling of the stories. Better still, if you live in an area where one of the major network news programs runs a half-hour before another network's evening news, you can have your child watch both programs on the same evening and make a list of the stories and the times devoted to each story on each network. If all the networks run their news at the same time in your area, you can record one network on an audio recorder while you watch another (if you have two television sets). By comparing two network news programs, your child will discover that editors differ in their priorities and that news reports can differ even when the story is the same.

- Have your child make a list of science stories in one week's television news. What is the basic science focus? What attitude do the reporters take toward science news?

- Ask your child to give a weather report for your area at that point in time. Have your child tell you the temperature, wind velocity, barometer and a forecast of what will happen in the next 24 hours. Then check with the TV weather forecast to see how accurate your child's forecast and readings have been.

- For older grade school children, it can be fun to have one or two children on teams take a position about some major news issue of the day and prepare arguments to support that position. Children could choose sides on some issue in the arms limitation debate and argue that side against the opposite approach. Much of the raw material for this can come from TV news.

Additional information can come for the local library.

- Discuss different kinds of government systems with your child, using countries in the news at the time (i.e., monarchy, democracy, dictatorship, parliamentary monarchy).
- Purchase an inexpensive world map or globe and have your youngster find the various countries on the map that are mentioned in the evening's TV news.

OTHER KINDS OF PROGRAMS

Besides programs specifically aimed at grade school children, such as "The Electric Company," "Studio See," "The Muppet Show" and various seasonal specials, television has a wide variety of programs that could become children's favorites depending on their taste, personality and maturity. Some children can't seem to get enough of sports programs, and this can be a particular problem for parents with cable television's ESPN Sports Network who want to limit their child's viewing hours. Some children may enjoy the afternoon interview and celebrity talk programs with Merv Griffin, Phil Donahue or possibly a local host. Finally, television's high number of quiz and game shows is a sure clue that they are popular with adults and children alike. You can make all the programs you allow your child to watch more valuable by getting your youngster to interact with them.

SPORTS

Communication ————————————————————

- Have your child watch a television sports scoreboard, then list the many different words the announcer uses to describe winning and losing teams in the course of giving the score. For example, one team "beats," "trounces" or "clobbers" another. At other times, it is simply one team "over" another. Is there some symbolism in any of these terms?

- Each sport has its own terms for plays, equipment and officials. A "referee" in football is an "umpire" in baseball, for example. If your child likes watching a particular sport on television, ask him or her to make a list of terms that are only used in that particular sport. Point out that some terms are used in more than one sport and some only in one sport.

- Invite your child to be a sports announcer at a make-believe game. If there are two children, one can be the play-by-play announcer and the other can provide background or color. Point out the difference between these two distinct jobs in television sports.

Creative Imagination

- Have your child draw the uniform for each favorite sport, coloring in the team colors for your hometown, school or professional team.

- See if your child can make up a melody that would be appropriate for a sporting event.

- Have your child compare the music from sports events to music from commercials, dramas, news and cartoons. Try making up some music for each type of program.

- Ask your child to listen for and identify the songs for various professional teams or various cities.

- Encourage your child to make up some sports trivia quizzes or games geared to the particular sport in season. Have him or her try out the game with playmates.

Critical and Evaluative Thinking ───────────────

- Talk about a game on television. Encourage your child to be a "Monday morning quarterback" and evaluate how well a particular game was played and why one team or the other lost.
- See if your child can compare and contrast the experience of watching a game on television and seeing one in person. Try to bring out some of the differences in these two experiences.
- Most sports involve some underlying science, but some are more clearly dependent on science than others. Ask your child to identify at least three sports in which science plays a prominent role (auto racing or skiing, for example). Have your child explain the relationship of the sport to science.
- Encourage your child to consider how the rules of the game make the sporting contest all the more interesting. Point out how many games are not only tests of skill between one opponent and another, but also between the players and the rules that confine and control what they can and can't do in the game.

INTERVIEW-VARIETY-TALK SHOWS

Communication ───────────────

- Point out various different mannerisms of talk show guests. Ask your child if some of these are distracting, and if so, why?
- Have your child pay attention to various accents of talk show guests. See if your child can identify where guests are from on the basis of their accent.
- When there's a particularly interesting guest who

speaks easily and well, draw attention to that person and see if your child can tell one or two things about the guest's way of putting words together that makes for especially interesting listening.

- On an early evening variety show, like a Bob Hope special or some other comedy show where a comedian delivers a monologue, point out how some of the humor relies almost wholly on unexpected turns of phrases, puns or other features of language. See if your child can identify two or three jokes that rely solely on language for their humor.

- In variety shows, even in shows like Merv Griffin, there often are songs and orchestral arrangements. Point out the different styles of singing and how different singers deliver a song. Some belt it out, others sing in a bluesy way and others almost talk out a song. Use these opportunities to introduce your child to different styles and approaches to song.

Creative Imagination

- Encourage your child and some playmates to play "talkshow." Have the children play the role of various guests, with one child playing the role of host. Alternate roles.

- Put on a variety show with singing, dancing, puppets and comedy. Get the whole neighborhood involved, kids and adults.

- Be interviewed as if you were a guest on your child's talk show. Tell about what you did that was particularly interesting recently.

- Encourage your child to design a variety show set or a talk show set. Make it as complex as your child's artistic talent will allow. Be sure to leave room in the stage area for the cameras.

Critical and Evaluative Thinking

- Ask your child to identify the kinds of achievements in the arts, sciences and sports that might make a person an interesting guest on a talk show.
- Ask your child to think up a question for each guest as if he or she were the show's host.
- Notice the skits in a comedy-variety hour. Ask your child to compare these to a typical situation comedy. Which is usually more topical, relating to the news of the day? Why?

QUIZ-GAME SHOWS

Communication

- Let your child play a quiz show host and get the family to play a simple version of a favorite television game show. If there aren't enough family members, suggest that your child invite some playmates over.
- Whenever your child is watching a quiz or game show, encourage him or her to play along with the game and try to answer the questions.
- You can play a whole lot of word games as if they were television programs, adding to the excitement in the process. Charades is an old standard, but even a simple guessing game about the meanings of new words can be fun for a child to play with you or playmates.

Creative Imagination

- Encourage your child to think up a game show idea that would work on television. If it's really good, send it in to one of the networks.

- An old radio and television game show that can be fun to play at home is "Name that Tune." See if your child can identify songs he or she hears by title. Or you can play records, hum or simply use theme songs from the television to see if your child can identify the title or the show they're from.
- Have your child make the props needed to play a simple quiz game — either one already on television or one your child has made up.

Critical and Evaluative Thinking

- If your child has a favorite quiz or game show, get some books from the library that might provide answers or background for the kinds of questions the show features, so that your child can improve at playing the game.
- Explain the difference between winning in a sporting event and winning in a quiz or game show. See if your child can explain the difference between mental and physical skill and between mental and physical exercise.
- Like situation comedies, many quiz and game shows are spin-offs from earlier successful ones. Ask your child to select two game or quiz shows that have many essentials in common and to explain the areas of similarity and difference.

Television also has many programs whose primary purpose is to educate and inform their audiences. Public television programs like "Nova," "Odyssey," "America" and the "National Geographic Specials" come readily to mind as memorable educational programs. Commercial television has its share of such programs too. Documentaries, travelogues, special reports, science programs and interviews like "Meet the Press" or "Face the Nation" teach, inform and enlighten. Children can easily spend more than an hour a day watching these kinds of programs and learning about our complex and exciting world from them. But even specifically educational programs need careful handling. Children who grow accustomed to learning from these programs can become educationally complacent and may well be easily bored by the slower pace of the traditional classroom.

You can help offset this by taking time after the program is finished to discuss what your child learned from it. Make the discussion itself a learning experience and a chance for your child to think about and analyze what he or she has seen on television. Make the program a resource, a focus for discussion and a kind of textbook rather than a self-contained educational experience. In that process you will put the program in its proper perspective. Children who find out early that real learning comes from quiet introspection and analysis will be far less likely to grow impatient with the classroom pace. Those who are unsupervised may suppose wrongly from their television viewing experience that most learning comes by simply sitting passively in front of the television soaking up information.

Even though your child can do various things with television to increase its educational benefit, you should still strictly limit a gradeschooler's television viewing, particularly on school days and evenings. One or two hours daily is more than enough television stimulation for a young mind. Youngsters need time for other activities that help them mature socially and mentally. And you should carefully screen the programs you do allow your child to watch for those two hours.

Some parents have found it helpful to ask their child to circle programs in the weekly newspaper television guide that he or she wants to watch each day during the upcoming week. This preselection process will make your child think about why he or she watches a program, and what programs are more important than others. If you stick to the preselected schedule, you can get, or keep, your child out of the habit of sitting mindlessly in front of the set.

During the grade school years, your child will be learning

to read, write and polish the social skills needed throughout life. But television is an aural medium, and children who constantly listen to television news, television drama, television sports, weather, talk shows and quiz shows are constantly hearing rather than reading or writing language. In one sense, exposure to language in whatever form is valuable for the grade school child, improving vocabulary, providing good pronunciation models and even supplying memorably well-turned phrases from time to time. However, there is an important difference in style between the spoken and the written word, a difference that children who constantly watch television will unfortunately not understand or recognize. Television can help your child most when it's balanced with other forms of intellectual recreation and stimulation — reading, writing and analyzing.

5

TEENS AND TELEVISION

In junior and senior high schools, teachers emphasize thinking skills, shifting away from basic facts and focusing instead on teaching children how to use facts as a basis for abstract and logical thinking. Algebra and geometry encourage students to think through mathematical processes rather than to just learn answers; in social studies students begin to explore both sides of issues and to realize that there can be more than one right position. In English, students look beyond the simple questions of what happened to inquire how a literary piece works as language and how it conveys cultural and personal meanings.

Even as junior high and high school teachers struggle to bring young minds to the next plateau of cognitive development, our American teenagers, according to A. C. Nielsen data, spend an average of twenty-five-and-a-half hours each week watching television. Even worse, teenagers continue to watch many of the same situation comedies and action adventure series they liked in grade school. Thus, our children are growing up with television programs that fail to grow up with them. Some situation comedies may present numerous exciting challenges for a three- or seven-year-old mind, but by age ten or twelve, your youngster has already mastered various language skills and become more socially adept. Therefore watching such programs becomes more and more passive; a source of little mental stimulation.

Parents who encourage their teenagers to think about what

they watch, question elements of plot, character or motivation in stories, recognize bias in news reporting and analyze the workings of commercials, can help to turn passive viewing into active learning. The silliest situation comedy can still provide raw material for your teenager to use in polishing the ability to question, analyze and evaluate. As we've seen with younger children, television programs can be used to teach a variety of skills.

Many of my suggestions require writing — an activity that teenagers get far too little of and one that can never be over-stressed. But if your son or daughter feels that what you're asking is too much like homework, you can minimize that feeling by suggesting that your youngster make rough notes instead of writing out a more formal piece. You can even just talk about his or her ideas together if that makes it easier to get things started; then you can gradually encourage your youngster to write down those ideas, even if only in an informal diary or journal form. The point of all the activities I suggest is to get your teenager thinking and writing about the programs, rather than watching them passively. Television shows can be a marvelous jumping off place for all kinds of analytical and creative thinking.

COMMERCIALS

Television commercials are slickly crafted arguments, thirty or sixty seconds long. Many commercials persuade by example. Mary had a headache until she took Bleepo. Now, only minutes later, she feels fine; you too will feel better with Bleepo. Some commercials argue from a set of semilogical principles: Gummo Motors builds a better car. You want to own a better car, so wouldn't you really rather have a Gummo? Still other commercials use some famous person to endorse a product, implying that the star wouldn't endorse a product if it weren't good or that the product advertised helped the star become a success.

Other commercials persuade by subtle visual or verbal suggestion. Janet, a grandmother who looks surprisingly well preserved and healthy, stops her tennis game long enough to tell us that she takes good care of herself. She eats properly, gets plenty of fresh air and exercise and takes Curtisol once a day. The commercial makes no claims whatever for Curtisol, but the implications are visually and verbally clear: If you take Curtisol, you too can be a young-looking grandmother like Janet. You could also be a young-looking grandmother if you have your first child at seventeen and if that child has children at an early age. But arguments don't always have to be logical to be persuasive. The art of persuasion has been pretty much the same since the time of the ancient Greeks. Only the products and the claims have changed.

Commercials work at both our conscious and our subconscious levels to make us prefer one product or service over another or to make us want something we wouldn't otherwise care about. Television commercials are usually more effective than persuasive arguments in real life because the commercials are so carefully constructed and because they add art and music to language for more impact. They're more effective as well because they're shown over and over until they are injected semipermanently into our memories.

Advertising agencies spend months of research before designing, writing and producing a thirty- or sixty-second commercial. Often more time and money is spent on a commercial than entertainment producers spend for a full half-hour program. Commercials don't just happen: they're carefully planned, tested and retested before you ever see them. Since the producers of commercials have studied all the classical and modern tricks of persuasion, you and your family should at least be aware of some of these same tricks so that you can protect yourselves.

Because advertisers don't want to offend any particular special-interest group, commercials deal in the stereotypical "average." Television commercials feature only nice homes and nice people in pleasant surroundings. We watch these scenes over and over and finally begin to believe that they do indeed depict life as it really is. But they don't. Commercials present a fantasy world where human problems are solved by simply changing brands of soap, toothpaste or deodorant and where most people are youthful, thin, handsome and well-groomed. Teenagers who watch television undoubtedly realize that the world of commercials is a make-believe world, but they might not have a clear picture as to why this is so. Discussion of the world that commercials depict, analysis of the methods commercials use and a full understanding of what commercials are trying to do to us can heighten your teenager's abilities to look beyond the immediate effects of commercials. These analytical and critical skills can also be invaluable in dealing with the real world in general.

Having watched nearly six months of commercials by age twelve, your youngster is experienced enough with the form to be a fairly good judge of what is going on. But the quantity of watching may not by itself improve the quality of watching. Teenagers need to learn how to analyze and isolate the techniques used in commercials. You can help your youngster improve these skills of analysis by suggesting some of the following activities and points of discussion, and by being willing to compare your own impressions of things you see on television with those of your teenager. You may even enjoy doing some of the things I suggest here, to sharpen your own critical skills.

Communication

- Have everyone in the family compete to see who notices grammatical errors in commercials first. Look especially for those purposeful errors that commercial writers use so that the slogan rhymes or is otherwise memorable. For example, "Homer Formby — no one knows wood as good."

- Select a commercial on a network evening news program and one that runs during a Saturday morning children's show. See if your teenager can determine if the words in one are significantly more complex or "adult" than the words in the other. If so, how, and in what ways do the "adult" words differ from the words in the commercial for the childrens' show?

- Encourage your youngster to keep a list of words that are particularly "commercial" — words that claim special value for the products, like "new," "improved," "bigger," "juicier," "fresher" and "handier." Use as many words on this list as possible to make up a commercial for some product or service. Will such a commercial, using many of these "commercial" words, be effective? If not, why not?

- Ask your youngster to write a comic parody of a commercial he or she particularly dislikes. What features are especially dislikeable? Make sure the parody takes those features to comic extreme.

- Have your teenager write a letter to a manufacturer either praising or criticizing a product. Make sure the letter contains specific details. Get the address of the manufacturer from the product package at the store and mail the letter.

- Ask your teenager to take notes on what are called "institutional" commercials. These are usually designed to inform us about research or product development activities that a particular company is involved in rather than to sell any specific product or service. Such commercials often run on public affairs programs or just before a network news program. See if your youngster can pick out words and other elements used that are different from words and the style of product commercials. What are these differences and how do they help "sell" the company name and image?

Creative Imagination

- Select an imaginary product or service and have your teenager create separate commercials to sell to (1) men, ages 18–34; (2) teenage girls; and (3) children under eleven. One might do this by recasting the commercial format for each group, using a cartoon commercial for one group and a movie star endorsing the product or service for another group.
- If your youngster wants some weekend or summer work, have him or her make up a flyer using television techniques to advertise a personal service he or she is willing to perform — lawn mowing, baby sitting, etc. Distribute the flyer in the neighborhood.
- See if your youngster can come up with suggestions for a local merchant to improve the sale of a particular product, perhaps with the help of some techniques that commercials use. Write this up and submit it to the merchant.
- Ask your teenager to write a radio commercial that will make people want to buy a service or product that no one needs. Now, adapt this commercial to television. What things will your youngster add to make the commercial more suitable to TV? Will the television commercial necessarily be more effective?
- Encourage your youngster to think of particular and specific techniques or arguments that would be effective with other teens in convincing them to use seat belts, avoid cigarettes, drive within the speed limit or some similar health or safety issue. Use these techniques to write a thirty-second public service message aimed directly at the teenage audience, then try the message out on some friends to see if they think it is effective. Your son or daughter may want to submit this to the local TV station.

- Encourage your teenager to make up a musical jingle for your hometown or school that uses the same basic techniques as commercial jingles. What are some of those basic techniques?

Critical and Evaluative Thinking

- Invite your youngster to select two commercials that offend viewers by haranging them or being overly repetitious. Try to figure out how they work and why they succeed. Remember, offensiveness is part of their design and technique.
- Ask your teenager to keep a weekly log of types of programs and the kinds of products that usually run commercials in those programs. See if there is a recognizable trend, and if so, what connections there are between the products and the show types?
- Help your youngster pick out one or two commercials that make absolutely no positive claims whatever for their product (Geritol commercials are a good example). Then have your youngster isolate the major techniques these commercials use and employ them to create a commercial for orange juice or tree bark tonic.
- Invite your youngster to select a commercial that operates primarily on the visual rather than the verbal level and list as many of those visual techniques as possible (for example, appealing color, attractive models, camera shots through soft-focus filters that make things appear dreamy and romantic and props). Perfume commercials are often a good choice for this kind of analysis.
- Acquaint your teenager with the uses of product packaging to sell products on television and at the store. Have your youngster go to the store and look

carefully at color, package texture and shape and any artwork on the package, including the product logo itself. Then write out some notes on why packaging alone can make one product seem more desirable than its competitor.

- Have your youngster keep a log of the sex, age, weight, apparent wealth and relative good looks of people who appear in most television commercials. What qualities, characteristics and stereotypes appear most often and what conclusions can be drawn from this?

STORIES OF ALL KINDS

In high school literature classes, students discuss plots or comment on characters, dialogue, setting, style or theme. In other classes, literary works serve as examples of cultural differences, ethical dilemmas, previous historical periods, different social customs and human relationships. Your teenager can practice this same kind of analysis using the wide range of movies, comedy and adventure series and even the literary classics that television presents. Again, the potential for learning is heightened if the viewer responds to the program and interacts with it rather than sitting passively in an electronically-induced stupor.

Dramatic presentations of every sort — comedies, action-adventure shows, movies, Shakespeare's plays and even cartoons — are made up of a plotted sequence of events or actions performed by characters speaking dialogue. On many television programs, as in many modern plays and movies, the story — the sequence of individual events or actions — is less important than the characters, the dialogue and the ideas underlying those words. In situation comedies and cartoons, for example, the comic dialogue and the opportunity for characters to interact in comic situations are both more important than the story itself. In fact, the stories are often terribly contrived and at times preposterous. You can help your teenager to understand better how these dramatic presentations are constructed by encouraging him or her to think about the basic elements in these programs (plot, character, dialogue, setting, style, theme) and to consider which element is most important in a particular show and how all of the literary elements fit together.

Notice, for example, that serious or comic programs aren't all drama and comedy. Often the moral or social message is so strong that it completely interrupts the flow of the program: Louise Jefferson holds forth on racial or marital harmony, the Fonz regales us with his live-and-let-live philosophy or Hawkeye muses about the insanity of war and the value of all human life. It's important for teenagers to recognize that even programs themselves have such "commercial" interruptions, when the message or the moral of the story takes precedence over the entertainment. This is not just a feature of television programs. It's done in novels, short stories, plays and movies, and our youngsters need to be able to recognize when it's happening. What they learn about television's manipulations (we can be manipulated for good as well as bad), they can readily apply to other media as well.

Communication

- Ask your teenager to select a favorite dramatic or comedy series and write a simple plot outline for a story that would fit into the series.
- Encourage your youngster to write a segment of dialogue between two characters in a favorite situation comedy. Ask if the fact that characters in situation comedies are basically predictable makes it easier for your youngster to write dialogue because he or she has a pretty good idea of what a particular character is likely to say in a given situation.
- See if your teenager can match up schoolmates, neighbors or family friends with similar personality

types in various television situation comedies. Then see how many literary characters (from Shakespeare, Twain, Dickens, Hawthorne and so forth) he or she can match up with TV character types. Do the television characters take certain typical human character traits to a greater comic extreme than exists in real life or in literary classics?

- Ask your teenager to note carefully the use of music in setting the mood in a dramatic production. Write an essay on the effect of music on the TV viewer. Turn this in as an assignment in a literature class.

- With every program that tells a story, whether serious or comic, you have an opportunity to ask your youngster if the story seemed far-fetched and unrealistic or fairly true-to-life. If unrealistic, you can probe further to determine if your teenager thought the story pleasantly or amusingly unrealistic, or simply unintelligently so. You can ask the question about the characters in the story and about the things they do.

- Have your teenager write a review of a serious television drama that he or she either liked or disliked. (Sometimes it's easier to review something you disliked). Ask your youngster to make this a very specific review and not just a statement that the program was good or bad. Remember that these kinds of programs are made up of the following structural elements, each of which should be well constructed in itself and should also fit in with every other element: 1) a *story* or sequence of events tied together by some cause and effect logic (but perhaps not very well tied together); 2) *characters*, either fully or sketchily drawn, and their motives for performing various actions in the story; 3) *dialogue*, the things the characters say to one another, which may or may not be always carefully adjusted to the character's personality; 4) *sets, scenery* and *costumes* (in any drama, movie, or television production even street clothes become costumes and are part of the overall effect); 5) a *theme*, or some kind of underlying social or ethical message; and 6) *music* (in most instances). The overall effect is also enhanced by the acting ability or inability, the style of the production and the sound, lighting and camera techniques. These can also be included as part of the overall critique. Encourage your teenager to include all or at least as many of these elements as possible in supporting the critique. Read, comment on and have your youngster polish and submit the completed work to your local paper, school magazine or some other publication. The finished work might also become a school homework paper.

Creative Imagination

- In an action–adventure show or other serious drama, have your youngster watch for specific camera cuts and other visual effects that add impact to the suspense or otherwise make the program more moving. Are some of these particularly unusual, creative or artistic?

- Encourage your youngster to think up comic situations that can be used in a favorite situation comedy. How does the show itself and its format, characters and theme limit the kind of situations your teenager can think up? Have your son or daughter develop a comic situation that might itself become the centerpiece for a new TV situation comedy and notice how it, too, puts limits on what will and won't work within its format.

- Suggest that your teenager write and produce an episode for a favorite TV series. Use neighbors, parents and younger brothers and sisters; get everybody involved.

- Ask your teenager to choose a good movie he or she recently watched on TV. Design a weekly TV dramatic or comedy series based on the main idea and charters of that movie. What elements can you keep? What characters would be regulars in the series? What would be the central, continuing theme?
- Have your youngster notice the acting in a show. Pick out the weakest actor in the program. What are the weaknesses? Are there problems with voice, stiffness of bearing or portrayal of emotion? Can we be sure the weakness comes from the actor and not from the role?

Critical and Evaluative Thinking

- In some programs, the locale is almost as important as the main characters, functioning as a unifying factor to tie the overall show together. This is true in shows like "The Little House on the Prairie" and "The Waltons," as well as in a comedy like "M*A*S*H." In other programs, the locale is relatively unimportant. Ask your teenager to list five programs (in addition to the three mentioned here) where locale is very important and five where locale is unimportant. Are there other differences between these two types of programs that result from their different treatment of locale?
- Select a program that dramatizes a well-known novel or short story — perhaps a movie or a PBS program like "The American Short Story." Make an audio (or video) cassette recording of the TV show and have your youngster carefully compare the television program with the original. Which did he or she like better? What characters in one are left out of the other? How much of the plot remains the same in both? Are subplots in the original (little secondary stories) cut

from the TV version? Ask your teenager to summarize the strengths and shortcomings of each medium.

- Suggest that your teenager compare and contrast word usage, humor, dramatic technique and the camera and sound techniques found in a British television program or movie with an American show that is roughly similar. Warn your youngster in advance not to oversimplify the differences, and encourage him or her to follow up with readings in the library about the differences between the two cultures.

- Discuss a movie or dramatic show you've watched with your teenager, particularly the social or ethical values the show presents or the main characters it depicts. For example, how would you characterize J. R. Ewing's social and business ethics. Is the world that "Dallas" presents realistic or extreme? Are there really people like J. R. in the world? What might it be like to work for a man like J. R.?

- Watch a dramatic presentation or documentary about some controversial subject with your teenager. Use the program as a point of discussion about the values presented. Instead of giving your ideas, try asking your teenager for his or her impression.

- Both small children and adults enjoy cartoons. Ask your teenager to select a cartoon like "Bugs Bunny" and identify the levels of sophistication and layers of humor in the cartoon that allow it to appeal to various age groups.

NEWS, PUBLIC AFFAIRS, WEATHER

By age twelve, most youngsters should be interested enough in current events to be regularly watching the evening news. If your home has cable television, your teenager probably also enjoys watching Congressional debates on C-SPAN and other specialized information services like the Weather Channel or the Cable Health Network. Local, network, public and cable television now provide more information about the world around us than most of our grandparents could have even imagined. Television brings this information with such ease that it has become the primary source of news and information for most Americans.

The strengths of television news are its immediacy, strong impact and ability to present sounds and pictures from anywhere in the world. The primary weakness is its compression of complex stories and issues into a limited time period with a resulting lack of depth and background. Television news is of course more than a headline service, but it seldom explores the levels of complexity that usually surround a major news story.

Equally important, television news is spoken, not written, and its language must be easy to understand. Newspaper readers can go back over and reread a section of a story that might have baffled or confused them the first time through. But television viewers have to understand the story fully the first time. To help them, television news writers shape language for the ear rather than the eye. As a consequence, television news language is repetitive and basically simple in grammar and word choices. Multisyllable words are rare and sentences are primarily in the simple subject–verb–object form. This simple "statement grammar" of television news is often simplified even more when announcers purposely leave out verbs. These verbless sentences sound important and urgent when spoken by an announcer, but they provide a poor example indeed for young writers: "Bad news in the economy tonight . . . . Interest rates up . . . wholesale prices up . . . employment down."

Because it is spoken, the language of television news is entirely different from that of newspapers. Youngsters who grow up watching television news without balancing it with extensive reading are likely to write in the oral style. They may seem to be shallow thinkers and awkward writers in school mostly because they are unconsciously following an oral model rather than a written one. Some of the activities I suggest can help your youngster understand the differences between oral and written language; other activities can help you and your teenager think about television news more critically and analytically.

It's important to remember that simply watching television news and public affairs programs is itself a learning experience. News teaches, and television news is particularly memorable because it teaches with pictures and sound. If youngsters supplement television's presentations by reading the newspaper or one of the weekly news magazines, they will have the necessary balance between the spoken and written presentation of the news, and will have the advantages of the immediacy of television news and the background depth that only printed media can provide.

Communication

- Encourage your teenager to listen for words that might bias a story, subjective words that reveal how the reporter thinks about a particular story.
- Using an audio cassette recorder, have your youngster tape a news story on television, transcribe it on paper then closely compare the differences between the television version and one in the newspaper. Of course the television story will be shorter and have less detail than the newspaper story, but there will also be important differences in language, style and storytelling techniques that your youngster should try to identify.
- Select some newsworthy event. Ask your youngster to write one story about it for television and another story about it for the newspaper, applying the information gained from the comparison between the two types.

- Encourage your youngster to compile a list of words and phrases that recur in television news stories.
- Again using an audio cassette recorder, have your teenager record a news story that uses film or tape extensively (as opposed to one where the on-air reporter merely tells the story in the studio). Wait a day or so, then replay the audiotape and note just how important the film is in making the story clear.
- Suggest that your youngster select an on-going story that will have to unfold over a period of a week or more. Keep a record of how it develops and particularly how the reporters handle that development and keep us interested in the story. Are there particular verbal transitions that set the stage each night and rekindle our interest in the story?

Creative Imagination

- Pictures accompanying a news story can add to or detract from a story. Ask your teenager to point out instances where the camera work sensationalizes the subject and other instances where it is wholly objective.
- Have your youngster pay special attention the next time the news includes freehand courtroom drawings. Ask your teenager to identify various techniques these artists use to capture the essence of the people and the scene with a few broad strokes, then make some drawings at home or school using the same techniques.
- If your school or community organization has a special newsworthy event coming up, encourage your youngster to write a "press release" about the event and send it to the local television station's news director. Follow up with a telephone call before the event and see about getting news coverage.

- If your teenager is at all interested in a career in television news, you can encourage him or her to write local or national news stories, weather forecasts or farm reports, and practice delivering them as they would be delivered on television.
- Suggest that your youngster watch two different network or cable news programs on the same night, keeping an accurate diary of the differences in lead stories, emphasis and time devoted to each story by each news organization. Ask your youngster to take on the editor's role. How would he or she arrange the stories, and why?
- Suggest that your teenager put together a still-photo essay on some community or school problem that could accompany a TV news story on the problem. Write the script to go along with the pictures, and send it to your local TV station's news director.

Critical and Evaluative Thinking

- Watch a documentary segment of "60 Minutes" or "20/20." Ask your teenager to rate the segment. Was it well researched? Was the segment presented objectively or did it use splashy sensationalism? Did the report present all sides of the issue?
- Select a documentary program like "CBS Reports" or the evening "MacNeill-Lehrer Report" and watch it as a family. Discuss the way the program presents the different points of view. Was there fairness? Was one side more convincing than the other? If so, was that because of the personality of the advocate for that position or simply because the position itself was more acceptable or the arguments for it more logical? Did the side you agreed with come out the apparent winner? Is that because you already agreed with that particular position?

- Ask your teenager to identify any logical or other relationship between news stories that follow one another in a news broadcast. Is there a theme or other device that holds some together? What transitional statements do the reporters make to move from one story to another? Is the only real relationship simply that one story physically follows another?
- Suggest that your youngster call the local television station's news assignment editor some morning to find out where and when a crew will be covering a press conference or other preplanned local news story. Take your youngster to the scene to watch how it's done. See if together you can identify the various pieces of equipment and the jobs of each member of the crew.
- Encourage your youngster to list the various devices that a station uses to make its news program more exciting than simply one or two "talking heads." These would include maps, charts, reports from the scene, film or taped segments, variation of the camera angle in the studio or switches between cameras.

SPORTS, INTERVIEW, TALK AND VARIETY PROGRAMS

You can encourage the development of language skills as well as analytical and critical thinking in your teenager with other kinds of programs, even ones that might not seem to offer much of an opportunity for learning. Here are a few ideas to get you started.

Communication

- Have your teenager watch a football, baseball or basketball game on television with the sound turned off and listen to the play-by-play on radio. What are the differences in announcing techniques between the television and the radio sportscasters?

- Have your youngster try his or her hand at writing an opening comic monologue for a talk show host. Point out how these are often topical and frequently refer to items in the news.
- Suggest that your teenager make up an interview with some famous author from the past — Chaucer, Shakespeare, Emily Dickinson — using the style of some famous talk show host and asking intelligent questions about the author's "latest" book.
- Take your youngster to a local TV station and be an audience participant in a talk show. Have your teenager write up the experience for the school paper.

Creative Imagination

- Have your teenager interview you about your job or something you've recently accomplished. Point out how talk show hosts can ask probing questions without being impolite. See if your teenager can successfully adapt that kind of style to the interview.
- Ask your youngster to make up an imaginary interview with a famous historical figure like Alexander the Great, George Washington or Queen Victoria, using the techniques of a well-known talk show host.
- Suggest that your youngster use a TV game show as a model and make up a game that can entertain the guests at an upcoming birthday party for a younger brother or sister or a neighborhood friend.
- Suggest that your teenager produce a variety show using neighborhood or family talent. Include musical performances, comic skits and monologues.

Critical and Evaluative Thinking

- Ask your youngster to explain why some sports are really enjoyable on television, but others don't seem to work well at all.
- See if your youngster can list three or four things that television does to control or change a game or other sports event that it presents.
- Select an in-depth interview program like "Donahue." Watch the program as a family and discuss the views of the guest and the way the interviewer brought those out. Are there techniques here that your teenager can adapt to talking with friends or acquaintances?
- Ask your teenager to analyze the interviewing process. How do interviews on these kinds of programs differ from reporters' interviews on news programs?

There are, of course, dozens of other activities you can have your teenager do with these and other television programs to make the programs more valuable as learning tools. The suggestions I've made here and in earlier chapters are just a beginning. They are a way to get you thinking about other similar activities and points for discussion. You can use old movies to discuss word usage, clothing styles and the manners and behavior codes of times past. Your youngster can play along with the quiz programs, matching wits against the contestants on the show or even with you or other relatives and friends. The important thing to remember is that whenever your youngster mentally interacts with television programs or uses a particular program as a jumping off point for discussion or other analytical or creative activities, the program becomes a learning tool. A little time-filling is acceptable, but make sure that your youngster doesn't let television viewing become a mindless habit.

6

AND WHAT ABOUT ADULTS AND TELEVISION?

Up to now I've been suggesting things you can do to make a child's television viewing an educational experience. Now I want to put the spotlight on you. How often do you sit mindlessly in front of the television, letting it lull you into a state of suspended animation? How often do you watch one silly program after another, too lazy either to change channels or even to think about what else you might do to occupy your free time?

My father used to get to that point after spending a number of very busy days at work. He would sit in front of the set in a semisleeping state, but wake up immediately if I tried to turn off the set or change the channel and insist he was watching the program. How many of us do the same thing, watching the television in a kind of waking sleep after a long, hard day, too tired to go to bed, too tired to turn off the set and too exhausted to think of anything else to amuse or interest ourselves? But what kind of example do we set for children when we use television this way?

Many of the things I've suggested for children to do with television — particularly in the chapter for teenagers — can be valuable exercises or activities for you as well, and in many cases I've suggested that you can do these things along with your youngsters. Now I'd like to present a few more things you can do with television to put it in its proper perspective for yourself and make your viewing more enjoyable and valuable.

Perhaps the most important thing you can do as an adult is to ask yourself why you watch television in the first place, and particularly why you watch each individual program. Do you watch because you really enjoy that program or because the set is on and there's nothing better to do? In short, do you watch out of habit or out of choice? Be careful here: You'll find that you don't like to admit that you watch television simply out of habit and you'll be tempted to find some other reason why you watch. If you do watch out of habit — and you're among the vast majority of American adults if that is a major reason — you can help to break that habit by joining your youngster and taking the weekly television schedule, circling those programs you want to watch and sticking to your original choices.

You can also help to break the habit by setting yourself a reading goal such as one novel or biography each week or two. Keep the book with you when you're watching television; you can read it during the commercials. If you've selected a good book, you'll usually find that it will be more interesting than the television show and that you'll stay with it even after the commercial break is over. Because television viewing is a passive activity, once you get actively interested in any other engaging activity, such as reading a good book or even the newspaper, there's little to entice you back to television. Television's demands on our attention are basically negative. Television attracts us mainly when nothing else does.

You can make those programs you do watch more valuable by joining your child in some of the activities I suggest and by thinking analytically about those programs you particularly enjoy. Asking yourself why you enjoy them and look at what makes them enjoyable for you.

Now let's review the same program types we've worked with in the previous chapters, this time thinking about some things we adults can do to make them a more valuable viewing experience.

COMMERCIALS

Advertising is an important source of consumer information. Even though television commercials are obviously biased toward a particular brand or service or merchant, they are often the first way that we find out about a new type of product or a new place to shop. Locally produced commercials tell us about special sales and new stores in the area. Imagine what life would be like without radio, television or newspaper advertisements. We would have to rely chiefly on word of mouth to find out who was having a sale or what manufacturers were introducing a new product or improving an old one. Whether we like them or not, television commercials are often our first source of important consumer information.

What we have to do is make sure that we use commercials as sources of information and minimize their persuasive powers. Here is a kind of checklist of things you can do to help achieve that goal.

- When you select some new product or brand, ask yourself if it is because you saw it advertised on television. If you answer yes, check your motives for buying the item now. Do you really want the product or are you actually responding to the commercial's suggestion?

- Every time you see a television commercial, try to summarize in your mind the basic argument used in the commercial. What are the primary reasons the commercial presents to urge you to buy the product or shop at a particular store? For a product, do the reasons concern quality, improvement, taste, power or other factors? For a retail outlet, do the reasons concern a better selection, price, quantity or convenience? Ask yourself if you really believe the basic argument or if it could just as easily be made about a competitor.

- Turn the sound off and look carefully at the visual images in a commercial. Notice what the pictures do to make the product or service attractive, and recognize that these are carefully controlled presentations of reality designed to influence your eye.

- When a commercial makes you feel that you really want the product, ask yourself precisely what the ad said or showed about the item that made you want it. Is your interest real or artificially sparked by the commercial?

Most of us don't watch commercials that closely, and that's one reason why advertisers repeat them over and over. After seeing and hearing about a product or store for weeks or months, it becomes familiar, and that makes us more likely to buy the product or shop in the store. We go to Smiling Freddie's Auto Repair because somehow we feel that we know Freddie. We buy a particular brand of toothpaste because we've heard about it for months and we remember its catchy slogan. Television commercials become a kind of subliminal "word of mouth" endorsement. We can minimize that effect by watching less television, thereby decreasing the number of times we hear about a product, service or retail store, as well as by consciously questioning ourselves before we make a purchase. You may ultimately discover that you are buying the product because of the commercial; the important thing is that you know you are.

STORIES OF ALL KINDS

All through our lives, we love stories. There is something basic about our delight in the narrative, whether tragic or comic, fact or fiction. In its mammoth demand for dramatic productions, television can't always be particularly choosey, and what we see is often second or third rate. Dramas can be weak in many specific areas, though television dramas are most likely to have contrived or forced plots and inadequate characterization, since these two elements are usually the most difficult to do well and in a hurry.

- When you watch dramatic presentations on television, ask yourself if the characters are believable and if what they do seems to have some kind of internal logic to it. If you find yourself thinking that what you're watching is silly or absurd, or that people don't really act like the characters in the television show, turn the program off and analyze it in detail. Look for stereotyping, simplification of issues and the way television tries, often heavy-handedly, to teach social values and behaviors.

- Purposely change your viewing habits for an evening. Choose your favorite viewing night and watch an entirely different sequence of programs. Tune to the PBS channel, for example, and at the end of the evening compare the differences between mass appeal dramatic television and the alternative fare on public television.

- Using the weekly TV schedule, select in advance a movie you want to watch that is based on a novel or short story. Get the book from the library. You can read the book before or after you watch the movie on television, and you should try it different ways with different movies. Since we usually tell ourselves a story best, you'll probably find that you don't like the movie as well as the book if you read the book first, and that you like the movie better if you see it before you read the book. The important thing is to become aware of the differences in story telling between movies and books, and to recognize the strengths and weaknesses of each.

- Be alert to the many times in serious action drama, adventure drama and comedy how often you are getting a mixture of entertainment and rhetoric. Sometimes a character will literally expound a particular point of view. Other times the approach is more subtle, with one character apparently convincing another of a particular position. Notice how often the political or ethical view seems overlaid or even imposed upon the story or the characters, sticking out

like a sore thumb and detracting from the normal, ex-
pected flow of the story.

Producers have designed most of the dramatic and comedy
series on television to reach so many different age groups, tastes
and levels of education that the programs most often please no
one fully. To reach the masses, television has to be a compromise medium and as such, most of its programs are near misses
at best. Because there is no such thing as a "mass viewer," each
of us has to fit our own taste to that of some imaginary average
viewer who supposedly represents all of us. The result more
often than not is a misfit. Television thus leaves many of us
vaguely satiated but largely unsatisfied.

One good way to find satisfaction, of course, is a return to
reading. When you select a good book specifically to your own
taste — mystery, western, classic love story, science fiction or
historical novel — you tailor your entertainment pleasure directly to your mood and interests.

Used wisely, television can certainly be an enjoyable part
of our overall entertainment mix, augmenting the pleasure we
can get from books and from a wealth of other leisure time
activities. When we expect it to satisfy all our leisure time
needs, television most often proves itself not up to the task.

NEWS, PUBLIC AFFAIRS AND WEATHER

Well over half of us now make television our primary source of
news, and television does an impressive job keeping us instantly
informed about major and even minor news items worldwide.
We have to remind ourselves constantly, however, that each television newscast is the result of many editorial decisions. Because television seems so immediate, bringing us directly to the
scene of major stories, it's easy for us to believe that what we
see on a television news program is a direct transfer of reality to
our television screens. Not true. Every newscast has been edited,

and the editorial decisions include questions of whether a story will be reported from the scene or told by the anchor person in the studio, whether the story will be told with or without film or tape illustration, how many minutes will be allotted to each story, the order of the stories in the total newscast and whether each particular story will need subsequent follow-up in days or weeks to come. You may well enjoy television news more if you take the time to think through what goes on behind the scenes.

- As you watch the evening news, consider what you would have done differently if you were the editor. Are you pleased with the amount of time spent on each story or are there stories you want to know more about? Do you think the network put the most time and attention on the most important story of the day? Try watching different network news programs to see which ones please you most often.
- Do you get the feeling night after night that the news anchor is biased toward or against the position of the President or the leadership in Congress on various issues of the day? Do you see signs of this in the amount of time devoted to particular stories or in the order or sequence of stories? Could it be that your bias comes because the position you agree with isn't presented as if it were the best position?
- Carefully watch one of the Sunday public affairs programs, such as "Meet the Press," "Face the Nation" or "This Week." Notice how some reporters defer to the guest but others are aggressive in seeking answers to pointed questions. It's interesting to keep track of how different guests avoid answering certain questions without looking as if they're "stonewalling."
- Forecasting the weather has always been a somewhat tricky business, although with modern radar and other early warning systems, weather forecasting is getting more accurate. Notice how your local or national

television forecaster loads the forecast with electronic gimmicks and impressive visual effects to make what is basically a mundane subject more exciting to watch. Keep a log of daily predictions and work an accuracy percentage for the different forecasters in your area.

Television can teach us a lot about the world we live in, but it can't teach us everything we need to know to be well-informed citizens. Again, television is only one ingredient in a mix that includes newspapers, news magazines, books, discussions with friends and colleagues and experience itself. When we rely too heavily on any one of these to the exclusion of others, we risk distorting and narrowing our view, depriving ourselves of the full picture.

OTHER KINDS OF PROGRAMS

For some reason, millions of American adults watch daytime soap operas on television, For those of you hooked on soaps, there are constant opportunities for you to exercise problem-solving skills, pop psychoanalysis and even to test your own moral and ethical value system against those of the characters in the soaps. The seedy world of soaps is designed to attract our curiosity and hold our interest often by its very banality. Wise parents will absolutely, completely and wholly forbid their children of any age to watch television soaps. Wise parents will avoid the soaps themselves, too.

The other programs adults watch on television — play-by-play sports, game shows, quiz shows, interview shows and talk shows — can all provide enjoyment, diversion and relaxation, depending on your individual taste and interests. For the same reasons that your children can get more out of watching television by interacting with it, you too can gain more from the viewing experience if you make an effort to get involved with what you are watching and avoid the temptation to sit passively in front of the set, soaking up everything without thinking. Of course there are those times when we can all use a totally passive diversion; an opportunity to rest our minds without sleeping and to idle without effort and television can then be a welcome companion.

Television can be an electronic friend as well. There is a certain comfortable predictability about television's weekly cycle of programs. And there's a pleasantly comfortable feel about television's seasonal cycles as well — baseball in the spring and summer, football in the fall and basketball after the Superbowl. Interview programs, too, feature some of the same guests two or three times a year, and we get the feeling we know them as well as the show's host. The older we get and less active we become, the more we look to television to fill certain voids.

As parents, we must remember the same things we want to teach our children. Television is just one element in a wide mix of media available to inform and entertain us. When we use television in moderation and balance the time we spend viewing television with other activities — reading, writing, talking on the phone to friends, playing, pursuing hobbies — then television assumes its proper place among the many forms of diversion and delight. In the world we live in today, it's good to know we still have some recreational choices. We certainly need them.

PART 3: Conclusions

7

FINAL WARNINGS AND A LOOK TO THE FUTURE

Never before in history has there been an educational tool as powerful as television, and never before has such a force been so often trivialized. The same medium that can bring us live pictures from the surface of the moon or from inside the rings of Saturn, also clutters our minds with competing claims about the absorbency of paper towels, the whitening of toothpaste and the protection of underarm deodorants. The same medium that brings us Pavarotti in "La Boheme" also descends to the indelicacies of the bedpan on the afternoon soap operas.

Because it juxtaposes news and documentaries with fictions and fantasies, television becomes both reality imitating art and art imitating reality. The line between illusion and fact constantly shifts on television: we see a real car wreck on the news and a half hour later watch a fictional one on "CHiPS." We watch police S.W.A.T. teams on the evening news flush out a half-crazed husband from his estranged wife's apartment, then see a fictional version of the same thing on "Starsky and Hutch." Television's technical facilities are now so good that we often can't tell from the quality of the picture or sound whether we're watching an on-the-scenes news shot or an incident in a dramatic series.

Imagine, if you can, what this immense variety of programs — some real, some realistic, some fictional, some factual — can do to the mind of a three-year-old. Think for a moment about the impact this constant stream of pictures and sound has on the impressionable psyche of a nine-year-old. What television says with pictures, our children want to accept as fact. Only after they've been disappointed by an ad for a toy that didn't live up to its image or by the sudden realization that what they thought was true was only a story, do our children begin to grow skeptical about television. What we don't know is how much that skepticism and all-too-early maturity affect how our children perceive and interact with family, friends and the real world around them.

The exercises and activities I've suggested throughout this book can help make your children more aware of what television is doing to them and sharpen their critical viewing skills. But these are only a beginning to get you thinking about other similar activities. And no amount of these can do the job alone. You also have to limit the hours your children watch television and take a constant interest in what you do allow them to view. And you must watch television with your children and share with them your comments, questions and adult insights and perspectives about the programs. Only then can you neutralize television's potentially harmful effects and maximize its potential for benefit.

IMPROVING THE QUALITY OF TELEVISION

Most of what I've been saying about television applies to programs already available either on network, cable or public television. But we shouldn't be content with trying to make the most of what we have now. Television can do better by all of us, and we should insist that the television industry try to do better. First of all, commercial, cable and public television should bring us many more high-quality children's programs specifically targeted by age group and designed to enlighten as well as to entertain. Children's programs should encourage the children who watch them to do additional reading, and there should be books available for children that retell the television stories, just as adult books parallel popular movies. Public television had a series called "Once Upon a Classic;" we need more programs like that, and the books that the programs are based on should be mass marketed. Other new programs should explore issues that concern children and teenagers — questions of family, growing up, dependence and independence, school, part-time jobs, love, marriage and careers.

In addition to giving us high-quality childrens' programming, the television networks should also start setting aside enough time to explain the background to each day's news. Ted Turner does that now with his Cable News Network, but two-thirds of us don't have cable television. The three commercial networks and PBS have cultivated our taste for news and information programs and it's shameful that the news they give us is so skimpy, superficial and at times sensationalized. Television news is still in the tabloid stage, but it has proven in previous times of crisis that it can be much more than a tabloid. Americans deserve more than eight minutes of information on the leading story of the day. It's time for television news to make the next quantitative and qualitative leap from telling us the news to explaining the news to us.

Finally, television should once again become the premier American showcase for our best and brightest dramatic, musical and dance talent. Early television had "Playhouse 90," "Studio One," "The Voice of Firestone," "The Bell Telephone Hour," "The Hallmark Hall of Fame" and variety programs like "Your Show of Shows" and Ed Sullivan's "Toast of the Town" that showcased American performers, playwrights and composers. Our children desperately need to see fine musicians, singers, dancers and dramatic actors again to balance the inordinately high number of athletes that television presents day after day. We need to reinstall the violinists, the singers and the artists as social heroes or our future will be empty indeed.

We may not always believe it, but we the viewers are in ultimate control of what television presents. Television is a mass medium, responsive to demand. It is the plebescite of rejection that the producers understand. When enough of us turn off some of television's horrid banalities, the producers cast about for something else that will attract us. That is what has been happening now for a couple of years. Network television viewing is down and PBS and cable viewing are up. The network executives still aren't sure whether this is because Americans are rejecting network shows, or whether we are simply being attracted by alternatives available now that weren't as readily available in the recent past. You can be sure that the problem is vexing some of television's highest paid executives and that television will be changing to cut its audience losses.

FUTURE TELEVISION

Though we don't know for sure what television might offer in the future, we can be sure there will be many more choices than we have now. The television industry is about to enter a new technological age that will allow it to bring us an immense new assortment of programs. It is safe to say that in the next ten years, television's impact on us and our families will increase dramatically, though that impact may not be in the form of network television as we've known it in the past. For one thing, cable television, which now connects to less than a third of all American television households, will be available to more than half of our homes in a few years. In most cities, cable will be able to provide two-way interactive communication between an individual home and the rest of the community, as well as providing fifty or a hundred television channels of entertainment, information, data, home security, health monitoring and other services.

In addition to cable's ability to expand our program choices, video cassette recorders will soon come down in price and size, allowing us to customize our viewing times at reasonable cost by recording programs when they're broadcast and then watching them when it's most convenient, or even by recording movies while we sleep that we can play back at our convenience. Video disk players too will be far less expensive and more readily available. Because the optical or lase disk has extremely rapid frame-search ability and can be linked directly to a computer, these can provide a kind of "command video." You'll be able to take a video disk tour of an art gallery, for example, pausing to look at a single painting or choosing — with the flip of a lever — which corridor you want to go down and which paintings you want to see close up. A newly revived record industry may well present its musical groups — popular and classical — on video disk so that you can see as well as hear your favorite recording artists.

In addition to these sources of programs, we now have programs available to us on the newly deregulated subscription television channels that are on the air in many cities and will be in many of the others soon. These will provide pay movies or sporting events, but some might even transmit specialized professional instruction or data like stock market reports, supermarket pricing information for comparison shopping and even electronic mail.

The FCC has also begun licensing a new class of low-power television station with small transmitters that can broadcast for a range of fifteen miles or so. These may well become television's version of local radio. For the next few years most of these stations will provide subscription movie services just like the full-power subscription stations, but if the video disk technology catches on and program products are available, it's likely that in a few years low-power television stations will have live disk jockeys playing those video disk recordings of the nation's top popular songs — interspersed, of course, with ads.

In the major cities there may also be multichannel microwave systems, wireless cable television, bringing news, sporting events, movies, fine arts and even hard-copy data printouts on up to eight separate channels to home subscribers. An experimental system is working now in Salt Lake City, and it is working well.

Satellites have already revolutionized the communications

industry. The growth of cable television from a community antenna system to pull in distant stations, to a program service with specialized news, sports, movie, congressional and health channels is a direct result of satellites and their ability to deliver programs nationwide inexpensively. The FCC has now authorized more than a half dozen companies to begin building and launching new higher-powered satellites that can transmit directly to small rooftop dish antennas, no more than a foot or so in diameter. These direct broadcast satellite (DBS) systems will each provide four to six channels of subscription or advertiser-supported channels coast to coast, most of which will completely bypass the local television stations.

Television stations in selected cities around the country are now experimenting with still another way of transmitting messages to us. A television picture is formed on the screen by an electron beam that moves from the top of the screen to the bottom, tracing 525 lines of information along the way. When the beam reaches the bottom of the screen, it needs time to get back up to the top so it can begin to trace another 525 lines on the screen. So you won't see a wild beam of light moving from the bottom of the screen to the top, there is a period of time during each of these cycles when the television transmitter sends no video picture information and the beam in your set cuts off. The technical term for this is the "vertical blanking interval," and you can see what it looks like if you make your picture roll out of vertical synchronization. This black bar at the bottom of your picture is normally unused, but now, with new technology, a television station can use this time which occurs sixty times each second to transmit all kinds of information. The information can range from newspaper stories to airline schedules, and users can select from a menu or table of contents simply by pressing numbered buttons on a control box hooked into a special decoder. A similar technology can deliver up to a million pages to your television set over the telephone, and this telephone-based service can operate in both directions; you can make airline reservations, order merchandise, send electronic mail over your phone to the computer and receive information from the computer over the phone. A satellite-delivered national teletext service is now available on many cable television systems as well.

Still other technology doubles the number of lines that make up the television picture. This "high-density television" (HDTV) can be delivered by specially designed transmitters, either on the ground or in satellite orbit, to sophisticated receivers at home. The effect is much like the difference between the high-fidelity phonograph record and the 78 RPM platter. High-density television brings television's clarity and resolution almost to the level of the theatrical movie or the 35 millimeter slide, and is particularly dramatic when used with projection television systems that produce six-foot, or larger, images.

All the technology needed to achieve everything I've listed is available now, awaiting consumer interest and demand to bring the unit price down even further. Also in place are the land and microwave links of your local phone company and A T & T. With the breakup of the Bell System into A T & T and various independent local operating phone companies, the telephone companies will be able to enter a number of new businesses, using their microwave and land lines to interconnect our home television sets with computer terminals and news and information sources, even full television communications over the new fiber optic links. The effects of these changes will be slow in coming, but they will be immense, affecting every aspect of telecommunications for decades to come.

So we now have the technology of the present, waiting for the users of the future. That is the irony of modern telecommunications at this juncture. Humanity now has more avenues of communication and channels open and waiting, than we know what to do with. Technology is ahead of the marketplace; the supply is greater than the demand. That's why cable television now provides us with more of the same kind of thing we already have on commercial and public television. Program creators haven't found something different enough that people will be willing and eager to watch. Even with this great technological advancement, movies are still television's main attraction, more than eighty years after their invention, and will probably remain so for at least the next decade.

But even though television in the future will probably give us more of what we have now, the very availability of so many movies, sports and news programs will increase television's allure for us and our children. Remember, too, that we'll be connecting our television sets of tomorrow to video games and home computers far more often than we do today. We are, in short, fast becoming a video nation, a people whose work, play and relaxation all involve some use of a television set. Our reality is becoming flickeringly phosphorescent.

There's not much any of us can do to try to alter the future. What we must do, however, is make sure that our children keep that future in its proper perspective. We need to encourage our children to read and write more. We need to make them literate in the new language of computers. And we need to make them literate in the television medium as well. Though it will become an even more powerful force in all of our lives in the decade ahead, we must make sure that our children perceive television as just one means of communication; one tool out of many available to us in the continual process of interrelating with one another. When we use television in moderation and handle it with care, it can be a valuable teacher, a wonderful friend and a good servant.

REFERENCES

I referred to a number of works in the course of preparing this book. Because I didn't want to burden you with a series of footnotes, I will cite here the following as among the most helpful in my research. They are listed in order of my reference to them in the text:

Television and Behavior: Ten Years of Scientific Progress and Implications for the Eighties, ed, David Pearl, et al. (Rockville, Maryland: National Institute of Mental Health, 1982).

Child and Teenage Television Viewing 1981 (New York: A. C. Nielsen Company, 1981).

L. H. Streicher, N. L. Bonney, "Children Talk about Television," *Journal of Communication,* 24 (3) (1974), 54–61; and P. J. Mohr, "Parental Guidance of Children's Viewing of Evening Television Programs," *Journal of Broadcasting,* 23 (1979).

M. Long, R. Simon, "The Roles and Statuses of Women and Children on Family TV Programs," *Journalism Quarterly,* 51, (1974).

George Gerbner, L. Gross, "Violence Profile No. 6: Trends in Network Television Drama and Viewer Conceptions of Social Reality: 1967–1973," unpublished manuscript. Annenberg School of Communications, University of Pennsylvania, (1974).

J. L. Singer, D. G. Singer, *Television, Imagination, and Aggression: A Study of Preschoolers* (Hillsdale, New Jersey: Erlbaum, 1980), and G. T. Ellis, F. Sekyra, III, "The Effect of Aggressive Cartoons on the Behavior of First Grade Children," *Journal of Psychology,* 81 (1972).

B. A. Watkins, S. L. Calvert, A. Huston-Stein, J. C. Wright, "Children's Recall of Television Material: Effects of Presentation Mode and Adult Labeling," *Developmental Psychology,* 16 (1980).

"The Viewing is Easy," *Channels,* April/May (1982).

David Saltman, "No Verbs Tonight . . . The Reasons . . . The Consequences," *TV Guide,* December 12, 1981.

SUGGESTED READINGS

In addition to the books, reports and articles I cite in the reference section, you can find articles about television that will help you and your family become more aware of the way the medium works in *Channels, TV Guide* and the television sections of *Newsweek* and *Time*. A number of interesting books are also available, and many of these, in turn, include further suggestions for reading. I list some here which specifically relate to children and television, to television's production and technical aspects and to the history of the medium.

Dorr, Aimée, and Palmer, Edward, ed. *Children and the Faces of Television: Teaching, Violence, Selling.* (New York: Academic Press),1980.

Barcus, F. Earle, and Wolkin, Rachel. *Children's Television: An Analysis of Programming and Advertising.* (New York: Praeger), 1977.

Brown, Les. *The New York Times Encyclopedia of Television.* (New York: Times Books), 1977.

Cirino, Robert. *We're Being More than Entertained.* (Honolulu: Lighthouse Press), 1977.

Greenfield, Jeff. *Television: The First Fifty Years.* (New York: Harry Abrams), 1977.

Howe, Michael J. A. *Television and Children.* (London: New University Education), 1977.

Jones, E. G. *Television Magic.* (New York: Viking Press), 1978.

Kaye, Heidi, ed. *Critical Television Viewing.* (New York: Cambridge, The Basic Skills Company), 1980.

Kuhns, W. *Why We Watch Them: Interpreting TV Shows.* (New York: Benziger Publishers), 1970.

Mankiewicz, Frank, and Joel Swerdlow. *Remote Control.* (New York: Times Books), 1978.

Moody, Kate. *Growing up on Television: A Report to Parents.* (New York: Times Books), 1980.

Postman, Neil. *The Disappearance of Childhood.* (New York: Delacorte), 1982.

Potter, Rosemary Lee. *New Season: The Positive Uses of Commercial Television with Children.* (Ohio: Charles E. Merrill, Co.), 1976.

Sandler, Martin W., and Peggy Charren. *Changing Channels: Living (Sensibly) with Television.* (Reading, Massachusetts: Addison-Weseley Publishing), 1983.

Singer, Dorothy, Singer, Jerome, and Zukerman, Diane. *Teaching Television: How to Use TV to Your Child's Advantage.* (New York: Dial Press), 1981.

Wehranranberg, Judith, and Winick, Mariann. *Children and TV.* (New York: Association for Childhood Education International), 1981.

Winn, Marie. *The Plug-In Drug* (New York: Viking Press), 1977.

APPENDIX 1

A SHORT COURSE IN BROADCASTING: 1982

[Reprinted, with permission, from the
1982 Broadcasting/Cablecasting Yearbook].

There were 9,092 radio stations operating in the United States at the end of 1981. Of these, 4,630 were commercial AM's, 3,346 were commercial FM's and 1,116 were noncommercial FM's. There were 1,042 operating television stations: 524 commercial VHF's, 248 commercial UHF's, 107 noncommercial VHF's and 163 noncommercial UHF's. Most commercial TV's are network affiliated; approximately two hundred operate as independents.

No single entity may own more than seven stations in each service (AM, FM or TV). In TV, no more than five may be VHF. No owner may have two stations of the same service in the same community. No owner of three VHF's in the top fifty markets may purchase other VHF's in the top fifty without a showing of compelling public interest. Newspaper owners may no longer purchase broadcast properties in the same market, nor may radio station owners acquire TV stations there, nor TV owners radio outlets. TV stations may no longer acquire cable TV franchises in the same city and networks may not own cable systems at all.

In 1980, the last year for which official FCC figures are available, commercial broadcasting had total revenues of approximately $12.0 billion. Profits were $1.8 billion. Television accounted for $8.8 billion (73.5 percent) of revenues and $1.6 billion (91.5 percent) of profits; radio, for approximately $3.2 billion (26.5 percent) and $154 million (8.5 percent). Public broadcasting had a 1980 income of $696.6 million — 27 percent from the Federal government.

There are more than 81 million U.S. homes (98 percent of all homes) with television sets, about 50 percent of which have more than one set. About 71 million sets are color. It is estimated that about 96 percent of TV homes can receive UHF signals, and that about 25 percent are linked with cable systems, according to Arbitron Television. There are an estimated 457.5 million radio sets in the U. S., 338.6 million (74 percent) of them in homes and 118.9 million (26 percent) out of homes.

The average American home watches TV for 6 hours and 45 minutes a day, according to A. C. Nielsen statistics. And the latest study by The Roper Organization (commissioned by the Television Information Office) shows that 64 percent of the U. S. public turns to TV as the source of most of its news and that 51 percent ranks it as the most believable news source.

The average 30-second, prime-time network television announcement now costs $100 thousand (spots on top-rated series cost $175 thousand; low-rated spots average about $45 thousand). An estimated 105 million people watched the 1982 Super Bowl telecast. Thirty-second announcements during that event cost $345 thousand. Thirty-second announcements on individual TV stations range from $15 thousand in top-rated specials in major markets to as low as $10 in the second-hundred markets. Radio spots cost from $600 or more in major markets to less than a dollar in small towns.

Growth of Broadcast Service

These tables show the development of broadcasting. The number of stations is as of Jan. 1 of the year noted.

Commercial radio in operation			Commercial TV station in operation			
Year	AM	FM	Year	Total	VHF	UHF
1955	2,669	552	1955	439	294	117
1960	3,456	678	1960	573	441	76
1965	4,012	1,270	1965	586	487	99
1966	4,050	1,446	1966	598	491	107
1967	4,117	1,631	1967	620	497	123
1968	4,171	1,779	1968	648	504	144
1969	4,236	1,944	1969	675	506	169
1970	4,319	2,184	1970	690	508	182
1971	4,323	2,196	1971	696	511	185
1972	4,355	2,304	1972	699	510	189
1973	4,393	2,482	1973	700	511	189
1974	4,422	2,605	1974	705	513	192
1975	4,432	2,636	1975	711	513	198
1976	4,463	2,767	1976	710	513	197
1977	4,497	2,873	1977	728	517	211
1978	4,513	3,001	1978	727	516	211
1979	4,549	3,104	1979	732	516	216
1980	4,559	3,155	1980	746	517	229
1981	4,589	3,282	1981	753	519	234

Noncommercial FM's in operation		Noncommercial TV's in operation			
Year	Total	Year	Total	VHF	UHF
1955	122	1955	9	—	—
1960	162	1960	44	—	—
1965	255	1965	88	54	34
1966	269	1966	105	61	44
1967	299	1967	118	67	51
1968	326	1968	146	71	75
1969	362	1969	172	76	96
1970	396	1970	182	77	105
1971	440	1971	196	85	111
1972	479	1972	206	89	117
1973	625	1973	229	91	138
1974	711	1974	233	91	142
1975	717	1975	241	95	146
1976	804	1976	252	97	155
1977	870	1977	256	101	155
1978	926	1978	259	101	158
1979	985	1979	260	102	158
1980	1,038	1980	267	105	162
1981	1,092	1981	268	106	162

APPENDIX 2

USEFUL ADDRESSES

ABC, The American Broadcasting Companies
1330 Avenue of the Americas
New York, N Y 10019
(212) 887-7777

CBS, The Columbia Broadcasting System
51 West 52nd Street
New York, N Y 10019
(212) 975-4321

NBC, The National Broadcasting Company
30 Rockefeller Plaza
New York, N Y 10020
(212) 664-4444

PBS, The Public Broadcasting Service
475 L'Enfant Plaza West, S.W.
Washington, D.C. 20024
(202) 488-5000

The Federal Communications Commission
1919 M Street, N.W.
Washington, D.C. 20554
(202) 632-7000